KU-353-574

LET LITURGY LIVE

Birmingham

W 5072034 1

LET LITURGY LIVE

A handbook of practical worship

OLIVER and IANTHE PRATT

SHEED AND WARD · LONDON

WESTHILL COLLEGE LIBRARY

14705

26 . 6 . 74

TS848 - £4.00

264

Copyright © 1973 by Oliver and Ianthe Pratt.   First published 1973.
All rights reserved.
This book is set in 11/12 pt. Linotype Baskerville, and printed in Great
Britain for Sheed and Ward Ltd, 6 Blenheim St, London W1Y 0SA
by William Clowes & Sons, Limited, London, Beccles and Colchester

Contents

CONTENTS

Prefatory note

It so happens that both the authors are Roman catholics. We have, therefore, gained much of our experience of creative worship among Roman catholics. It is our belief, however, that the general principles of making liturgy meaningful apply regardless of denomination. This book is addressed, therefore, to christians generally. Readers, whether Roman catholics or not, should bear this point in mind and we are confident that they will find little difficulty in taking account, where necessary, of special circumstances or denominational customs. Denominational differences have indeed steadily become less marked in recent years.

There are a very large number of people, clerical and lay, of different denominations and in various organisations, who have worked with us on various worship projects and tried out experimental services and without their help this book could never have been written. In particular we would like to thank for their comments, criticisms or contributions, Helen Bisset, Peter Bostock, Bernard Braley, Laurence Bright, Christine Butler, Stephen Burnett, Martin Chatfield, Tove Cullen, Pauline Groves, Janice Hendey, Roy Hill, Tom Hinds, Michael Ingram, Norman James, Nicholas Lash, Anthony Lovegrove, Geoffrey Preston, Robert Sharp, Kenneth Todd, Christopher Vallins, Lala Winkley and Joan Winthorpe.

Our children and those of our friends have also contributed by helping to prepare and try out children's services.

Finally we are much indebted to Thyrza Morris and Muriel Yates for their secretarial help.

1

Introduction

This book is about worship, the worship of the one church for which Christ prayed and upon which he sent his Spirit; the church that is always coming into existence, new in witness, worship and life; the church through which the Spirit lives and works among mankind.

A church that is a sacramental sign of Christ, a pattern of God's love through which the Spirit can enter human society here and now, will need forms of worship that are open to the Spirit, that will express the mission of christians as 'a royal priesthood, a holy nation', expressed in Vatican II by the emphatic use of the phrase 'People of God'. This is not all. We also require forms of worship that serve the needs of an outward-looking church, that bring together the gospel and the world and help us to see each in terms of the other. This means that our worship must develop a greater degree of flexibility to enable it to relate to the actual situation of any particular christian community. Something more than participation is needed to achieve this. The Spirit must be enabled to work in and through us by a new creative approach derived from a review both of where we stand in the world and of how we see and interpret the gospel.

That is what this book is about. It is not for people who want a guide for their private spiritual life in which their personal salvation is the main thing. On the other hand neither is it intended for people who think the problem is simple, and for whom being a christian means no more than going out to help the poor, feed the hungry and so on, with an occasional prayer for their needs.

This book is for people who feel a tension between the need to understand salvation and find the living Christ, at the same time as they carry his gospel to all mankind, whom he willed to draw into his saving act. Creative liturgy is for people who want to love God *and* the world, pray *and* work, finding the living Christ by working with others in the human situation, being in the world but not of the world.

Worship and the future of the church

Worship of its very nature reflects this duality. Thus, the eucharist is both the kingdom of God given to men and a call to them to work towards its realisation. The church is and has been, from the very beginning, a eucharistic community, whose members know one another and Christ in 'the breaking of the bread'. In this community christians walk as pilgrims on a path that leads from the promise of the last supper towards its fulfilment.

Thus, worship is part of God's plan, serving the needs of the church, his people. Worship bears closely upon the church's work and mission in the world, on the life and witness of all christians. That is, worship serves an outward-looking church that exists 'for others', adapting the gospel message to the needs of a rapidly changing world. Worship that helps christians do all these things will play a part in shaping the future development of the church and deciding the nature of its mission. Worship will change to meet the needs of a developing church and it cannot therefore be considered in isolation. To know how worship must develop one must know how christians live, the problems met in their daily lives, how each family, group or parish is answering the gospel call. Only when the way people are going is clear can decisions be taken about how worship should develop. Creative liturgical development should serve also the needs of missionary activity, bringing the agnostics around us towards belief. There is no real place in this sort of approach for liturgical reform as an end in itself.

A changing church, a church in crisis, must draw new life from liturgy, ie from the organisation of worship. Liturgy must help renew the church as it is finding its new shape, indeed help bring that new shape into being. We come together to praise God and thank him for all our blessings and as a body to find our identity, our distinctive character, to express our life and existence as a community of christian people, the people of God, doing his work. Liturgy is a means to enable christians to survive as a distinctive group, enabling us to hold on to what we believe, what we have in common with one another and indeed to express and give deeper meaning to those beliefs. Liturgy is essential, therefore, to the survival of the church.

Liturgy is important, too, as a means of finding Christ in the modern world. It is a continuing link with the age of the apostles, bridging the chasm of time and keeping alive the traditions of the early church and the gospel revelation. This does not mean that liturgy should be any sort of museum piece, rather in the way that one particular form of the Roman mass was used almost unchanged in the western church for many centuries. Tradition must be made to live by drawing upon the riches of the past so as to understand them in a new developed way, meaningful for the age in which we now live. Liturgy enables different races, nations and cultures to draw upon a common heritage, just as the church itself stands above frontiers, races and cultures.

Liturgy as the work of the Spirit

At the local as well as the global level worship enables people with differing views and outlooks to come to a better mutual understanding under the guidance of the Spirit (Jn 4 : 24). For example, Roman catholics who feel that many of the changes in their church since Vatican II have gone too far, losing something valuable of the past, can meet with those who feel that the essentials of Vatican II have not yet been put into practice and that much more radical changes are still needed. Worship should help these people to find common ground and see how to work together, tolerating differences. An encouraging example of how this should work was provided by the way many Roman clergy and churches found it possible to give people communion into the hand or on the tongue, standing or kneeling, as the people individually found most helpful. Many Roman catholics (accustomed from childhood to kneel and put out their tongues) would be hopelessly distracted from a proper prayerful attitude if compelled to change. Equally, others conscious of the eucharist as a re-enactment of the last supper, a shared meal and a participation in Christ's sacrifice derive a sense of its reality as a meal and of the immediacy of Christ's presence by a literal following of the injunction to take and eat. The clergy serve well the spiritual needs of the people by administering communion in the way that is most helpful to each individual.

Liturgy also provides an opportunity for the Spirit to teach people, helping them to understand the scriptures and, above all, if it is the sort of creative liturgy considered in this book, people will learn by taking an active part in making worship progressively more relevant to what they are doing as christians. In the first centuries, liturgy and catechesis were closely linked together and should become so once more.

Worship is important to the church today especially because it can help the church develop to meet the future, often for example finding ways round problems that look to be insoluble in purely human terms. If ways forward can be found, the theorists and theologians can follow later. Sometimes liturgy can project an image before us of the church of the future, so that we can begin to see what shape it should take. It is, so to speak, being worked out in principle. For example, in the ecumenical field as we work out how to pray and worship together with our fellow christians, a sort of blueprint emerges of how the church could be brought closer to that unity which Christ prayed that it should achieve.

There has been in the recent past a rather static period in liturgy when for several hundred years practically nothing happened. This was really dreadful but we who live today are fortunate. Even if we find it at first a little disturbing, we are catching up with arrears of liturgical development. We are living through a period which is rather exciting. It is difficult to realise it as we live through it, but what is really taking place is a new outpouring of the Spirit. New ways of cultural expression are being worked out in liturgy, music, drama, extemporary prayer, dancing and the use of people's own culture in worship. All this is only just beginning and we are on the brink of a period of new and rapid development, comparable for example with what happened in the fourth century, when the great festivals of the christian year took shape.

4

The experimental approach

Abstract intellectual discussion of liturgy has only limited value. There is only one way of finding out whether a new development in worship will serve better the needs of the church—that is to try it out and deliberately assess the results. During the 1960s the church authorities became progressively more willing first to tolerate and then to undertake and give their blessing to liturgical experiments. (See, for example, Vatican II *The sacred liturgy* 44, and *Preamble* to *Report of Church of England Liturgical Commission*, London 1966.) The liturgical achievements of the second Vatican Council were only possible because early Roman catholic pioneers in the field had already had the courage to experiment at a time when such action was formally forbidden and often met with official opposition.

This general principle remains valid today. In liturgy the prime need is for courageous, enlightened but *critical* experimentation. This means also that we must not accept uncritically what we are given, for example, in the way of new prayers, whether it is the latest collection published by our favourite devotional writer, or what we are given officially. Thus Roman catholics had in succession at the end of the nineteen-sixties a new set of mass collects, new forms of the eucharistic prayer and a new standard form of the mass. A critical examination both of official and of experimental material can help people to see what is needed and prepare them to write their own prayers applicable to the particular circumstances of their lives. Such critical efforts form part of the search for truth, a means of developing a worship that is honest and sincere, rather than one that only expresses what someone once felt that people ought to feel (whether they ever actually did or not). It runs parallel with the need for integrity in the church, that is of avoiding the dangers of triumphalism or of glossing over defects.

How to create a living liturgy

We must try to make liturgy more relevant and meaningful. There are two lines of approach. One is to start with the ordinary parish mass. Sooner or later, however, difficulty will be experienced because the people are unfamiliar with liturgical principles or are apathetic. It will be difficult to get active participation or a full response. Nobody but the clergy will want to take the initiative.

The other line of approach is to start by working with small groups. These may be family groups, catechism classes, St Vincent de Paul meetings or youth groups; in fact any sort of group or even individual families in their own homes. Groups will already contain the keen, capable people of the parish. It will be possible to give them individual help, the people will learn more rapidly, and special liturgical forms can be used which are adapted to the needs of whatever group is involved. The difficulty here will be that in most parishes only a small fraction of the parish will be touched by such measures and the overall effect will be limited to an élite. It will all seem a little pointless.

The fact is that neither of these two lines of approach is likely to work on its own. They both need to be used together and in such a way that they complement one another. To start with the groups can provide a nucleus of lay people, understanding something about liturgy, which will be the basis of participation for the parish congregation, and a means of breaking down the apathy amongst their fellow parishioners. On the other hand, once things get going in the parish, the people in the groups will begin to see the point of the liturgical experience that they are gaining. The groups will provide, too, a proving ground for new ideas before they are tried out in the parish as a whole.

The aim of this book is to provide a practical handbook to help forward this renewal of worship at different levels, dealing with both theory and practice, which must develop in mutual interaction. Starting from prayer and the spiritual life the problem of giving worship meaning in terms of the missionary role of christian communities will be examined from a variety of aspects. Then various forms of services are given, not necessarily to be used as such, but as means to illustrate how to develop and create a living liturgy. Finally a select list of easily available source material, much of it quoted in the text, is provided.

The usage of the word 'liturgy' in this book
The word 'liturgy' appears in the new testament where it
refers to the worship carried out by gatherings in a particular
place (eg Acts 13 : 2), according to its literal Greek meaning,
'the work of the people'. In contrast, some modern writers
have used the word in a narrower sense to refer to the official,
public worship organised by the church (eg Gregory Dix,
The Shape of the Liturgy, London, 1945, p 1). The word
'liturgy' is used in this book with its broader traditional meaning, to include all christian communal worship, thus avoiding the need to use such vague expression as 'para-liturgy'.

On this basis 'liturgy' includes such things as a short service
at the end of a meeting of an interdenominational house-
group, or a prayer meal celebrated at home by a family and
their friends. Such things may be done well or badly, like any
other sort of worship, but it is wrong to treat them as non-
liturgical (ie second-class) worship.

It is true that liturgical worship by definition is open to all
the people and carried out on behalf of the whole church.
This means that all christian worship should be carried out
on behalf of all believers and this can be done equally in
parish or family worship. Thus, a eucharist at 7 am on a
Monday morning in a parish church is intended for the
people of that denomination in that locality who find the
time a convenient one. The situation for the worship in the
interchurch house-group where christians meet to discuss
their mission in the local community is different only in
detail. Both examples are done on behalf of all christians and
are liturgical.

Neither is it just the 'official' worship of any given church
that is liturgical. To limit it in this way would stultify all
development and change, leading eventually to a museum-
piece liturgy unrelated to contemporary needs. Strictly speaking, liturgy cannot be 'official' or 'authorised', for the christian church did not exist first and then later decide to have an
official worship. On the contrary, the church exists primarily
as a worshipping community, 'breaking bread together':
the people of God are the people who worship God together.

The only worship that really constitutes the action of the

church is what people do, what they find helpful, whether in cathedrals, churches or small groups. This is not to say, of course, that there cannot be agreed guidelines, basic liturgical forms on which to build, and standard versions of commonly used prayers, but these things should positively help people and certainly not exclude new developments or local adaptations.

Liturgy does not always have to be 'public'. In general and in principle it will usually be so but during periods of persecution in the past the worship of the church had of necessity to be private. Most of the forms that we are concerned with in this book can be used either for public parish worship or less publicly in smaller groups. 'Less public' is a better description than 'private', for few groups are really private. Rather they are 'selective', for the commitment to carry out some apostolic task or mission necessarily involves the selection of members with a special interest, vocation or ability appropriate to the project that is being undertaken by the group. Thus when some forms are used primarily in special situations or by small groups, they are for 'specialised' rather than 'private' use. This means, for example, that the family should not exclude the friend or neighbour who wants to join them for worship.

Worship is praising God for his creation and thanking him for all our blessings. This can be done in different ways, in the home as well as in the cathedral. The definition of *liturgy* that we have adopted in this book is that it is the worship of God by the church, carried out by any group of the church's members.

It is the church, the christian community, that worships. But what is the christian community if it is not christians who work and worship together? Thus worship is an important way of defining or identifying a christian community. A small group at worship is usually readily seen to be a community. In contrast, it may be difficult to find any sort of community in a 'dead' parish with indifferent worship. Yet the worship of the group may fall short by being inward looking; the community may be too narrow a one.

There are two ways to help make sure that worship belongs

to the church: the 'official' universal community should concern itself with the particular local situations, and the local selective group should look outwards to the overall general situation of the church. Both ways have a role to play in liturgy.

2

Prayer in the modern world

It is surprising that so little attention has been given by theologians to the subject of prayer, for there are many problems to be solved. Primitive people asked God for rain but the sophisticated modern world knows too much about meteorology. People today ask if those who pray are trying to make God change his mind or if they think that he has after all overlooked something? Too often the language of public prayer is stilted and unreal. Personal prayer often looks like a way of withdrawing from the world and its problems that men ought to be able to solve but do not. There is a real danger that prayer will be rejected by many devout people as part of an obsolete and unhealthy pietism. Yet a cursory glance at scripture is enough to show us that christians are called upon repeatedly to pray and that a clear example of prayer was given to us, above all, by Christ himself. We cannot really work our problems out without expressing them in prayer any more than people can think effectively without using words. We cannot be proper christians without praying. We shall look at the role and meaning of prayer in the modern world as the most useful introduction to liturgical practice.

The nature of prayer
The first problem to be considered is what prayer is and why we pray. The following answer, given by a priest, seems to be a good one: 'I would say that prayer is a dialogue between myself and God, through Christ, in unity, in the Holy Spirit, with other christians in the church.' In other words, prayer is more than just a personal matter between the individual and God, but at the same time it necessarily involves God and is not just christians speaking to one another. One trouble

with this sort of definition is that the common experience of prayer that ordinary people have is that of a monologue rather than a dialogue. The emphasis on prayer as a 'conversation with God', nevertheless, has been widely used by spiritual writers. Prayer of petition places the conversation in the correct sort of context, of the created being approaching the creator, or of the adopted child asking the father for help. The difficulty that this seems to be trying to coerce God really relates only to the time before Christ. The Word become flesh has now entered into the human situation. The Jesus who wept over the coming destruction of Jerusalem can be asked as a human being to share our everyday problems in much the same way that we sometimes ask for the sympathetic help of a good friend (cf Karl Rahner, *Theological Investigations* III, London 1967, 209–210).

A rather different view of prayer from the conversation-with-God one is the utilitarian view. Paul Van Buren, for example, says: 'The meaning of intercessory prayer is its use: it begins in reflection upon the situation in the light of the christian perspective and leads to appropriate action.' (*The secular meaning of the gospel*, London 1963.) On this view prayer stems from concern for our neighbour and forms part of the sharing of our brother's burden. The christian will look at the world, for example, as if he were reading with his newspaper in one hand and his bible in the other. This is how he prays, looking at the world in the light of the gospel and the gospel in the light of the world: he not only talks to God but also has to find God's answer for himself. This process should guide him in taking the action that is needed.

Does this view make better sense in the modern world? Less emphasis is placed upon God but it is a more challenging and difficult approach. It is easy to pray for food for hungry Africans and Asians but difficult to work out how to sway public opinion and put enough pressure on governments to make them divert sufficient resources from space and military expenditure to make it possible to provide food for the hungry of the world.

The scope of prayer

As soon as one goes beyond the simple definition of prayer as talking to God, it becomes difficult to decide exactly what is or is not prayer. In liturgy, more easily than in private prayer, use can be made of poetry, drama and debate, things that have a teaching role without being prayer in the ordinary sense. Prayer may not always be immediately recognisable as such, especially on informal occasions as in the family. A young child may ask, for example, when his elder brother is unkind to him: 'Why do I have to forgive him?' The explanation given by the parent may well include an account of how Jesus has won for us God's forgiveness for our own sins (just like Daddy forgiving the children when they do dreadful things). Quite naturally such a talk will end with the parent asking the children to thank God for forgiving them and saying something like: 'Let's hope that God will help us all to learn how to forgive one another.' Such a statement, while not formally addressed to God, nevertheless brings him firmly into the picture and is a prayer in meaning and intent. Such situations do not always lead naturally to explicit prayers and to try to force formal prayers into such situations may only defeat the real purpose, which is to teach children how to think about God's will and to train them to have a prayerful attitude to life.

It is easier to make prayer explicit when it is asking for something. This is true not only for children but also for those on the fringes of the church who do not make a habit of prayer. As every parent knows, children find it easier to ask for something than to say a 'thank you' for it. Whether explicit or not, and whether we call it prayer (in a broader sense) or just a prayerful attitude, what must be explicitly recognised is that such occasions have a very important function as a means of relating liturgy to life and of making prayer meaningful in the modern world.

Private prayer and liturgical prayer

A division has grown up, especially since the middle ages, between private prayer and public liturgical prayer. The evidence of scripture and of the early church suggests (as we shall see below) that too sharp a division here is a mistake. The division has been sharpened by the rather personal concern of spiritual writings like those of John of the Cross or Teresa of Avila and the *Imitation of Christ*. It has been made worse too for Roman catholics by the liturgical use of Latin for so long after it was no longer understood by the people. The sharp contrast between liturgical and individual prayer for them was exemplified by private confession in the old days, when the penitent made his confession in personal terms, asking for God's forgiveness, and was given a formalised Latin absolution.

The division between individual private and public liturgical prayer is becoming progressively less sharp: in practice in both these fields we are concerned with different aspects of the same problem. As we learn to make liturgical prayer effective and meaningful, so shall we be able to use this to make individual prayer more fruitful. On the other hand, people have to learn how to pray at the individual personal level before they can play a creative part in public prayer. Indeed, useful lessons for liturgical prayer can be drawn from examples of individual prayer in the new testament, for the one is closely related to the other:

> Sing the words and tunes of the psalms and hymns when you are together, and go on singing and chanting to the Lord in your hearts, so that always and everywhere you are giving thanks to God . . . (Eph 5 : 19–20).

Prayer in the new testament
One of the best guides for prayer is the new testament. Paul, for example, frequently intercedes for the local churches, 'It is my prayer that your love may abound more and more' (Col 1 : 9). He asks us also to pray constantly, giving thanks to God 'in Christ Jesus' (1 Thess 5 : 18). He stresses the inadequacy of our prayer but says this should be no obstacle to us, for the Spirit himself will express our plea and God will know what is meant (Rom 8 : 26–27). This, incidentally, should provide encouragement for people trying out new liturgical forms if their initial efforts lack professional polish. In later writings, Paul prays to the Father, through the Son,

13

especially for the Spirit to be given (eg Eph 1 : 15–23 and 3 : 16–21).

The gospels show us a Christ constantly at prayer—at the baptism in the Jordan when the Spirit descends upon him; all night on the hills before calling his apostles; at the transfiguration; in the garden of Gethsemane and, above all, at the last supper. On many of these occasions he calls upon his followers to join him in prayer (eg Mk 14 : 32–40; Mt 6 : 9; Mt 7 : 7–11; Jn 14 : 13). The prayer of Christ is the prayer of God's people that in principle, at least, is that of a community, not just of one person. This is why he says 'Our Father' not 'My Father'. Sometimes he prays for himself or for the needs of one or two particular persons (as he does when performing some of the miracles) but more usually he prays for the whole church: 'not only for these' (ie his apostles and disciples) 'but for those also who through their words will believe in me' (Jn 17 : 20).

Another characteristic of the prayer of Christ in the gospels is that very often it is eschatological, ie it looks to the future fulfilment, as in 'Your kingdom come' or to the working out of God's will, 'Your will be done', to the blood 'that is to be poured out for many' (Mk 14 : 24) or to the cup that Jesus would like to pass but only if 'as you, not I, would have it' (Mk 14 : 36). Finally there is the prayer for all the faithful, that their unity may bring the world to believe and that Christ's followers may join him in heaven (Jn 17).

Yet another characteristic of the new testament treatment of prayer is the emphasis on sincerity. The ostentatious public hypocrisy of the Jewish religious leaders is denounced by Christ (Lk 18 : 11; Mt 6 : 5–6). Prayer is to be based on faith (Mk 11 : 22–24) and persistence is needed (Lk 11 : 5–8; 18 : 1–5). Christian prayer is to be like life within the family, for we are the adopted children of the heavenly Father (Lk 11 : 9–13).

Prayer as a search for truth
Another aspect of prayer that is seen in scripture is that of reflection, of 'pondering these things in one's heart' (Lk 1 : 66; 2 : 19, 52). Christ himself is depicted in the gospels as praying

with the aim of helping the spectators to understand better. When, for example, he raises Lazarus from the dead, he says:

Father, I thank you for hearing my prayer.
I knew indeed that you always hear me,
but I speak
for the sake of all those who stand round me,
so that they may believe it was you who sent me.

Why, indeed, should Christ pray publicly at all? He who was the Lord of creation and could work miracles would hardly have needed to ask for help. Presumably, he had an ordinary personal human need to pray, but the only reason for doing so in public seems to have been to give his followers an example and to help them to understand what was happening, that is to probe more deeply into the truth. Such an approach is rather like Paul Van Buren's utilitarian definition of prayer quoted previously (see p 11). Prayer is a way of making possible interaction between a person's experience of the situation and his knowledge of the christian perspective. Its basis is the new commandment of love, especially of one's neighbour. It is worth noting how often in the gospels prayer is linked with the forgiveness of sins and love of one another (eg Mt 5:43–44; 6:14–15; Mk 11:25; Lk 18:13; Jn 17:26).

A practical obstacle to the love of one's neighbour, in whom Christ himself is to be seen, is one's emotions. Such feelings as resentment, possessiveness, fear, hate, greed, wrongly directed love or feelings of inadequacy can be serious impediments to doing what is God's will. Prayer may well be a useful means of overcoming emotional barriers like these and developing personally a fully mature christian attitude so as to live more fully in Christ. The interaction that takes place in prayer makes possible the full growth of the human personality. It is all too easy to keep the religious and emotional aspects of one's life in separate compartments.

The social aspects of prayer
By this interaction prayer can reach areas of truth that cannot easily be reached by other means. The basis of the interaction is rather broader, however, than Paul van Buren's definition

suggests. It is not just between the secular situation as represented by our neighbour's material needs and the christian perspective as set out in scripture. An adequate description of what prayer is and does can only be expressed as an interaction between two different levels of understanding of the whole of our experience of life. Our total experience at the human level, including the needs of ourselves and others, and our inter-personal relationships, has to be cross-checked with our understanding of our experience of the world in the context of God's will and of the divine plan of salvation as revealed in the scriptures. Love of our neighbour naturally plays a big part by giving purpose to the process of interaction in prayer.

Thus prayer is a community-determined activity. There are other reasons, too, why prayer is not normally just a matter between the individual and God. One reason is that the basic work of prayer can be done best as a group activity. The interaction between our ordinary human experience and our understanding of things in the context of God's plan of salvation depends to a very large extent upon sharing our experience with that of others. It is in this way that we make sense of that experience. It becomes real for us. The well-known phrase of Descartes: 'I think, therefore I am' should perhaps be rendered in the light of modern social science as: 'I communicate, therefore I am.' To spend six months alone in a cave or sailing the oceans single-handed leads to severe psychological stress, whereas to be an effective member of a small group and to pray with them helps to maintain our sanity and our grasp of reality.

Is prayer answered?
There is more to it than that. Prayer is not just a monologue, nor does it really go unanswered. Prayer formally addressed to God is shared by our fellow men. It leads to appropriate action, which looks like mere action of human beings, but should really also be seen as the work of God. The Spirit is working in and through the human situation. Thus prayer, though formally a monologue, is really a multiple conversation in which God incarnate in the human situation does play a part. Prayer is at one and the same time human beings

speaking to God and God speaking to human beings. To a large extent this process can be described as a search for truth and an effort to do the will of God.

We are now, therefore, in a position to say that prayer is indeed answered. We are not concerned here with the possibility of a miraculous intervention but only with the question of whether there is a subjective answer to prayer. It is futile to look for an answer in the ordinary sense of a dialogue, but there is an answer all the same. It comes insofar as truth is more fully understood or God's will more closely followed. It is necessarily a partial answer for it comes through human agency and is, therefore, imperfect but, all the same and within these limitations, it should be seen as God's answer.

Openness to the truth

This understanding of prayer makes clear the need for an open attitude. The truth when found may be unpleasant. A truly penitent attitude is a willingness to face the truth. As things start to go wrong in a human way prayer must bring about renewal, that is a return to the original truth of the gospel and to finding ways to give it meaning in the present age. Prayer is the basis of leadership in the church. It must help leaders to find the truth and the rest of the faithful to accept the truth in freedom. Prayer is one way of sharing truth and, therefore, a basis of prophetic leadership. A leadership that ignores these principles or does not know how to search for and share truth is not acceptable, and such a state of affairs inevitably leads to a crisis of authority in the church. When this happens the prayerful search for truth is replaced by casuistic and apologetic attitudes. In the moral field, for example, people will ask questions like: 'How can I do what I want without a formal lie?' or in the field of theology: 'How can an argument be adduced in support of this belief?' The general overall effect of all this in the church tends towards a withdrawal from the world and a glorification of the church itself, glossing over its defects. The underlying cause of this situation is a lack of real holiness among christians. The only effective remedy for the situation and for difficulties of this sort is an attitude of openness and a search for truth through prayer.

Pentecostalism—the charismatic prayer movement

An important development in the 1970s in the communal use of prayer has been the movement of charismatic renewal taking a wide variety of forms—charismatic prayer groups, catholic pentecostals, *Focolari*, Jesus people, liberated christians and African independent churches. Scores of thousands of such diverse groups have in common the idea that christian life can be renewed by opening oneself to the free movement of the Spirit and by taking the gospel seriously.

This movement at best is much more than a new mix of emotionalism and fundamentalism from the past. The basis for renewal comes from the new testament accounts of the early church in which a personal change of heart and a personal baptism in the Spirit leads on to a commitment to renew church and society.

Charismatic renewal is particularly widespread among Roman catholics in the United States, starting among theologically literate university lecturers who felt they were lacking in the fire and love of God shown by the early christians. It now has many thousands of followers, finding less opposition in the Roman church than in other major churches, and even has cautious episcopal approval from the American hierarchy. Pentecostal 'parishes' have been set up in some places. One Canadian bishop has witnessed to those involved in pentecostalism within the church as developing a deep sense of the presence of God and his effective action in their lives. The catholic pentecostalist movement soon spread to Britain especially in the form of charismatic prayer groups.

Prayer in the church has for many centuries been polarised into formalised prayer and private individual prayer. At the prayer meeting the needs of the freedom of the individual and the strengths of community meet. Much prayer together may be silent, but there is a strong sense of community that develops and the individual is free to contribute his own spontaneous prayer to the group. The members pray together in faith, believing that all things are possible, for it is God who prays, works and acts through them. Reflecting on the gospels all pray for the baptism of the Spirit with a readiness to accept and use in their lives the gifts that will be given. Even if no charisma are granted a common experience within these groups is a feeling of joy and peace and many hours may be spent in prayer together without the participants flagging. One characteristic of these groups is that those taking part are often seized with an experience of the reality and goodness of God and that the prayer of praise, which ordinarily is one of the least used forms, arises spontaneously.

There are dangers as well as possibilities for great good in the movement. It grew rapidly from its inception in 1967 because it met a genuine need and it looks as if it will help to shape the future of the church. It is essential, however, that groups avoid degenerating into mere emotionalism and lack of concern for the community at large. Many of the most successful American groups have in fact pioneered new ways of meeting the needs of the secular community around them.

Doubt and faith
One problem that faces people in prayer, as well as when they want to experiment in worship, is the extent to which *doubt* should be expressed in prayer. If our individual prayer and also our worship is to be about the actual human situation and express people's real feelings and problems, doubt cannot be ignored. As well as hopes and fears, joys and sorrows, people have moments when the basis of their belief is far from certain. Such feeling may range all the way from a minor difficulty, like that of understanding how the accounts of an event can vary in different gospels, to a feeling that the church is so unholy that it is not really worth remaining a christian.

Prayer has to be honest. It is futile to try and suggest that such difficulties and doubts do not sometimes afflict even devout people. Nor is it much use suggesting that a difficulty has to be met by a blind act of faith of the kind: 'the church says this is so and therefore you must believe it.' Ordinary people react like Lewis Carroll's Alice:

> 'I can't believe that!' said Alice. 'Can't you?' the Queen said in a pitying tone. 'Try again: draw a long breath, and shut your eyes.' Alice laughed. 'There's no use trying,' she said: 'one can't believe impossible things!' 'I daresay you haven't had much practice' said the Queen.

Any problem that we try to treat in this sort of way merely

builds up trouble for the church in the future. Many of the most pressing problems of today come from difficulties that past generations tried to pretend did not exist or pushed underground by blind acts of faith in the name of obedience or loyalty. The existence of doubt or difficulty has to be recognised and probably ought, therefore, to find some sort of expression in prayer and worship. On the other hand one has to avoid the liturgical expression of doubt becoming purely negative. There is no difficulty about honestly facing the disbelief of the world, and even our own difficulties or doubts in private prayer, but what expression if any should we give to them in liturgy? The disbelief surrounding us has to be recognised as, for example, Matthew Arnold in his poem *Dover Beach* saw in the ebb and flow of the surf something like the waves of doubt and unbelief that were steadily eroding the structure of the medieval christian faith. In some modern christian folk songs these sorts of thing are expressed, for example, in 'Friday Morning' or '2,000 years' (Sydney Carter, *In the present tense* II and Malcolm Stewart, *Gospel song book*). In order to decide whether and how it can serve a possible constructive purpose it is worth looking at the place of doubt in scripture.

Doubt in scripture

The accounts of the early history of Israel and the writings of the prophets are full of human weakness and of failure to live up to the precepts of the law of Moses. Doubt in the modern sense is seen in the wisdom books, perhaps typically in Job with the concern of the writer with the problem of why the good were afflicted with suffering and why the wicked often seemed apparently to prosper in this world?

When we turn to the new testament it is not surprising to find little expression of difficulty or doubt in Paul, for he is close to the events of the life, death and resurrection of Jesus. The issue is simple: 'If Jesus be not risen we are still in our sins' (1 Cor 15 : 17). When the gospel traditions came to be written down, some of the closeness of the salvation events had gone. The purpose of the writing down was to try to preserve the memory of them, of the witnesses who had 'seen and touched and heard' (1 Jn 1 : 1).

There is the simple difficulty, for example, of Mary's: 'But how can that be for I have not known man?' There is the refusal of Thomas to believe in the risen Christ until he had put his hands into the wounds. In general, all such incidents are used to teach people something. An explanation is called for or a point has to be made. Doubt is expressed as part of the process of trying to understand, of seeking for the truth.

Paul gives an indication of why there is doubt when he says: 'Now we see in a glass darkly, then face to face' (1 Cor 13 : 12), stressing how limited our understanding and knowledge of things in this world is, being of necessity partial, imperfect and incomplete.

In scripture we have seen how doubt is a stepping stone to a deeper faith. So it should be too in prayer and in worship. For example:

> We can't believe in a Son of God
> Two thousand years away,
> But only in a Son of God
> That we can see today.
> (Sydney Carter, *Faith, Hope and Nativity*)

This should help us to understand the importance of making Christ's presence in the world real for our fellow men through the witness of our lives. It brings us to the practical problems. With our new understanding of the nature of prayer what can be done to make constructive interaction more likely? What can be done to help ensure that prayer leads to appropriate action?

A practical approach to prayer and worship
The best place to start is with the small group of keen people meeting regularly in someone's house, such as a family group, interdenominational group for christian renewal or, best of all, a group engaged in study of the bible. The first session should be devoted to trying to answer the question: 'Why do we pray and what do we expect the result to be?' Then the various views put forward in the earlier sections of this chapter can be discussed.

The next step is to look at the problem raised by trying to work out prayers to fit today's needs. This can be done by making a critical assessment of a collection of half a dozen or so contemporary examples of prayer. These prayers can be chosen from books that have proved to be useful sources for creative liturgy, or from prayers made up by other groups like themselves. They can be collected by the group themselves or they can ask some experienced person to provide them with a suitable collection.

The examples of prayers chosen by one such group included an extract from a prayer by Michel Quoist about the gospel being terribly easy to hear preached but very difficult to live, and about our fear of all the things that living it would mean. Then there was an extract from a prayer in poetic form by Brian Frost, unpublished at that time, about what drives people to take drugs (*Citizen Incognito*). The next example was a poem by Sidney Carter that begins: 'Your holy hearsay is not evidence, give me the good news in the present tense' (*In the present tense*, 1), subsequently set to music. There was an extract from a prayer about the church, that it should serve God rather than be treated as 'ours' (Caryl Micklem, *Contemporary prayers for public worship*).

There were also two examples of experimental prayers worked out by other groups working on experimental liturgy. One was a modernised version of the Roman 'I confess', and the other was a litany worked out previously for an experimental penitential service.

Critical assessment of contemporary prayer

The group that looked at these examples of modern prayers made various criticisms. The passage chosen from Quoist was thought to be too individualistic for the Anglo-Saxon temperament (the word 'I' occurred in 13 out of the 18 lines) and too emotional to be generally acceptable. The general theme, that the gospel demands more than I can give, was thought to be over-pessimistic in view of the meaning of *gospel* as 'good news'. The work of Michel Quoist has been very useful in showing that contemporary prayer can be used in liturgy but it was felt that there was plenty of room for other approaches.

The poem by Brian Frost was felt to be quite different. He tells us something about life, in this particular extract about how young people come to take dangerous drugs. He then goes on to look at this problem in its context in a prayerful manner:

> Lord, sometimes we need an escape
> From the pain of pressure
> built up right inside us;
> Bring back to our pained minds
> When we feel we need release
> The knowledge that you have,
> the secret of abundant life.

It was felt that this sort of treatment has an advantage by contrast with Quoist, who often packs so much into one line that it cannot easily be followed in liturgical use, for instance:

> I should give everything till there is not a single pain, a single misery, a single sin in the world,

is lost as one line of a prayer and in addition, because of its exaggeration, is likely to provoke a reaction.

People either liked the Sydney Carter poem a lot or not at all. It is spoken in dramatic form by an outside agnostic and addressed to christians, but it can be adapted for liturgical use, or used as it is. Various other criticisms were made of the prayers, especially of the expression of good ideas in language that was too flowery, or difficult to understand. Generally, prayers composed by other practical liturgy groups were liked as being simple and expressing the sort of things that people really feel.

This was a very valuable exercise giving the members of the group a useful insight into the sorts of problem involved in writing effective prayers for liturgical use. In fact, this group did go on to do some useful creative work itself and, in all probability, the personal prayer life of its members was enriched by their experience.

Making your own prayers for use in worship
Many people are hesitant about composing their own prayers for public use. This is understandable, especially among Roman catholics, who have only had experience of this sort of work since the end of the 1960s. There is also the problem of whether ordinary people *can* write prayers or whether only

a few specially trained people with a gift for colloquial writing can do it. Thus, there are two extreme viewpoints about this issue. One is to encourage people to say things in their own words, however unpolished the results may be. The other is to look out for the occasional poet who can express the people's ideas in their own idiom. Some compromise must generally be accepted between these two extremes.

There is also another issue to be resolved. This is whether our first need is to express the truth of the gospel and the events of salvation in the people's own idiom, or alternatively to let people pray, starting from their own problems as they experience them in their daily lives. In view of the previous discussion about the nature of prayer, it would seem that both these aims are reasonable and complementary, but that the second one may provide a better starting point in present circumstances because of the recent tendency to neglect the social aspects of christianity. When we pray we are not just talking to God. We are making use of an accumulated reservoir of personal and communal experience to see a way forward in the love of our neighbour and in the communicating to other men of christian teaching.

Thus it is feasible for a group of keen people of only ordinary ability to write their own liturgical prayers. Here is a brief summary of the procedure that we have outlined above:

1 The group should have a discussion about the nature and purpose of prayer.
2 They should collect together some examples of contemporary prayers and assess them critically.
3 They should construct their own prayers, starting from a consideration of the problems that concern them in their daily lives, looked at in the light of the gospel (with bible study in parallel if possible).
4 They should try these out in actual worship together.
5 They should assess, finally, how useful the prayers have been.

3

Children and the sacraments

The christian community maintains its identity through its worship and its sacraments, however much the practical details may vary between the different denominations. New members are admitted into this community, joining different churches within it, through a general process of initiation in which there are specific liturgical landmarks. These are the actual rites of initiation (baptism and confirmation) of which baptism is shared by all christians, and the point at which an individual first takes part in the sacramental life of the community (first communion, and for some, first confession, that is confession of sins in private, with absolution). Some or all of these events must take place at some time between birth and adult life. Widely differing views about the actual timing have been held by christians living in different centuries or owing allegiance to different churches. Practice in the matter has an important bearing upon the way in which children are introduced to the sacraments and to liturgy and on the manner in which they are instructed about the christian faith.

For some of the free churches, the problem does not exist in this form. The baptists, for example, only admit adults to baptism and the eucharist, the only sacraments that they recognise. For the 'catholic' churches where infant baptism is the general rule, the problem takes the form of deciding the order and ages at which children are confirmed and make their initial confession and communion. For anglicans there is the additional complication that confirmation has been treated as the rite that initiates to eucharistic communion. Private confession is open to those who find it helpful as adults.

Historically there have been wide variations in sacramental

practice. In the early church quite young children received communion regularly, as is still done in some eastern uniate churches. This remained fairly common in the west until the eleventh century when greater emphasis was placed on receiving the sacrament with reverence. The fourth Lateran Council laid down that the obligation to go to confession once a year and to receive communion at Easter should begin with 'years of discretion'. Theologians at the time considered this point was reached at the age when the child could decide between good and bad to the extent of being *doli capax*, ie capable of deceit. This was understood to mean the ability to commit mortal sin, and it was held at the time that this capacity developed at about seven years. The obligation to go to the sacraments from the age of seven was not strictly followed. There are references to children making their confessions from seven years onwards, but they do not appear to have communicated until several years later. Aquinas held that true devotion is necessary for the reception of communion and that this cannot be expected before ten or eleven. Until the eighteenth century it appears that it was fairly general practice for Roman catholic children to go to confession for some years before making their first communion. A real change come with Pius x who criticised the over-emphasis on reverence and the practice of different ages for first confession and communion. The obligation to receive communion was to begin at the age when the child began to use his reason, 'that is about the seventh year or a little later or even sooner'.

Canon 854 of the 1917 Roman catholic *Codex* laid down that the eucharist should not be given to children who by reason of age 'are unable to know and desire this sacrament'. If a child is in danger of death he needs only to be able to distinguish the eucharist from ordinary bread and to adore it reverently. Otherwise children need to know 'those mysteries of the faith which are absolutely necessary for salvation' and should approach the eucharist devoutly 'according to the capacity of their age'.

An exploratory survey of opinion
Following the second Vatican Council many Roman catholics

in Britain came to feel that the customary practice of introducing children to the sacraments, that is to first confession followed by first communion at about seven and to confirmation a year or two later, left much to be desired. The family apostolate committee of the Newman Association, a Roman catholic organisation of graduate and professional people, received a number of letters about this subject from distressed parents. It became evident, therefore, to the members of this committee (including the present writers) that it would be useful to collect the views and experience of parents and of other interested people on this problem.

The survey was an exploratory one carried out on a relatively modest scale, based on written and verbal views contributed in the late 1960s by some 200 people, members of family groups, married members of the Newman Association, the Grail and the Catholic Peoples' Weeks, by individual parents and by a small number of clergy and teachers.

The people were asked for their views about, and experience of, the eucharist, penance and confirmation in relation to children. The practice of infant baptism was taken for granted and this sacrament, therefore, excluded from the survey.

First communion
It was generally felt that parents should play a much greater role than in the past in assessing the readiness of their children for first communion (and first confession). It was pointed out that the parental role was stressed in canon law but often ignored in practice. Canon 854 runs that the decision of a child's readiness for first communion 'belongs primarily to the confessor and to the parents' but this is interpreted as the priest having a general supervisory role rather than having to be consulted on each individual case (cf Bouscaren Ellis & Capello, in commentaries on canon law).

Apart from one or two teachers who doubted the ability of parents to judge the readiness of their children, the vast majority of those giving their views placed the responsibility squarely on the parents, even if their conclusion was often qualified by the need to consult and for the parents to be well prepared to undertake this responsibility. Typical of the comments received was 'given suitably instructed parents, the whole responsibility should rest on them'.

It was felt by many people that teachers were in a better position than the clergy to assess a child's readiness, as the clergy, apart from those with special catechetical training, were not trained to understand the child and his special needs. There were, however, a considerable number of parents who expressed disquiet that teachers in the schools that their children attended were not using modern catechetical methods and were preparing for their first communion and confession in a way that was harmful to the proper religious development of the child.

It was suggested by many people that ways should be worked out for helping parents to prepare their children themselves. Some wanted much more of the preparation to be done by parents, 'the parental role ideally would be to take on the preparation aided by the teacher', others held that the parents' role in assessing the child's readiness for the sacraments and helping him prepare for these largely depended on the interest and intelligence of the parent and that many would need help in fulfilling this responsibility. This might be done through parent-teacher associations, greater participation in the family group movement, home visiting etc. The problem here is often that those who most need help will not come to meetings. Although normal responsibility should rest with the parents, clergy or teachers may have to step in where the parents are not able or willing to play their proper part. It was felt that many parents would have a better idea of the child's religious understanding and response, and therefore of his readiness for the sacraments, than the teacher, who has to deal with large classes.

There was a strong feeling that there should be an individual assessment of each child, although some held that there should be a general framework of rules with very flexible application, and some felt that there would be chaos without rules. Many parents commented on the different ages at which their own children had been ready for communion and therefore suggested that it was inadvisable for a whole class to make their first communion together. One group, however, felt that, except for exceptional circumstances, it was not wise that a child should be singled out from the class for earlier or later communion. Children do not like being different, but this difficulty would not arise if there was no standard age at which first communion was made by the whole class.

It was pointed out that the trend in secular education was away from class teaching towards greater emphasis on group and individual activity, a form of teaching which is more demanding on the teachers but where the child is more actively involved in learning at his own pace. Such methods should be the main ones used in the catechetical field. There is a considerable body of evidence that a catechesis based on the parish rather than the school is much more effective and it makes for greater flexibility.

An over-legalistic approach to first communion must be avoided. In the past too much emphasis has been put on rules regulating the approach to sharing the body of Christ. It is easier to teach rules than relationships but better that the child should be encouraged, as far as he is able, to see the sacraments as loving encounters with Christ. The approach that sees the eucharist as the family meal of the christian community where the people come together with their Lord and with each other needs to be stressed.

First confession
The majority of people answering the questionnaire felt that first communion and first confession should not be linked together for this perpetuated the idea that confession is necessary before each communion. It was felt also that the moral sense of the child was not sufficiently developed around six or seven for him to be able to commit a serious sin. Further, if a child gets into the habit of formalised confession of trivialities he may never grow out of it. The point was made that the sacrament of penance was generally unsatisfactory in its usual form and should be modified to make it more suitable for the young child. Another factor was that the communal aspect of penance had not been sufficiently emphasised in the past and needs to be brought back into our understanding of the sacrament, but that at a young age the

child has little or no sense of community and will not be able to understand this aspect.

On the other hand some people felt that the children need to get used to going to confession before the scepticism, embarrassment and problems of adolescent sexuality develop in the teens.

The idea of seven as the 'age of reason' came in for a great deal of criticism as a concept unrelated to fact. Most people favoured eight or nine as the age for the first confession and six or seven for first communion. A number of parents wrote bitterly of their experience of children being forced by their school to make their first confession before they were ready for it and of the child's fear of the confessional. Some parents found their children took to confession naturally and easily at seven; others reported discussions in the family on the question where the teenage children said they liked to feel clean before communion. One parent spoke of confession as a 'spiritual toilet' before communion, others by contrast spoke of children so terrified of their experience of first confession that two or three years later they had not been able to go back. The variation in experience indicates the need for a flexible and child-centred approach so that the individual makes his first confession at the stage most appropriate for him.

Children and the sacrament of penance

General dissatisfaction was expressed in the responses with the present practice for both adults and children. It was felt that much needs to be done to make this sacrament a more fruitful encounter with Christ and a real means of conversion or repentance. A typical comment was:

> The emphasis on a recital of faults, which in many cases do not vary from 7–70 years of age, and lack of analysis of motive and circumstances leads to an ineffective use of the sacrament.

There was an evident reaction away from the legalistic approach of categorising lists of sins into mortal and venial. It was felt that it would be an exception for a committed christian to commit a grave sin and that children did not have the necessary emotional and rational development personally to reject God in their actions. The need was felt for confession to be much more informal and consultative as well as less frequent.

A number of suggestions were made for making the practice of penance more effective. Clergy should be specially trained to take children's confessions. Possibly there could be one special children's confessor in each deanery who could visit the various parishes. There was also strong discouragement of old methods of teaching (some schools were still teaching about hell to six-year olds) and the restraining of older teachers.

In addition it was felt that the awareness of the meaning of penance should be developed for both child and adult in a community setting by a specially worked out liturgy, such as school and parish biblical services of penance.

It was felt that oral confession was not necessarily the best means for bringing about a searching of conscience and a deliberate turning back to God, and that people should be free to use either the confessional box or receive absolution in a community service of penance which gives time and stimulus for a true rethinking and recommittal to God. Many adults, let alone children, find the confessional repugnant and embarrassing and are unable to use it fruitfully. Others find it a help. Each individual has his own needs, and imposed uniformity means that the potential spiritual development of many is thwarted.

In some dioceses children communicate at seven and during the following year start taking part in non-sacramental confession services before the major feasts—these are geared to the child's needs and used for the formation of conscience. The next year they are introduced to the sacrament of confession through a communal celebration which emphasises the sacrament's social character—only in the following year do children start making private confessions, at the age of ten.

Confirmation

There was near unanimity in the answers that the early age customary for receiving confirmation by Roman catholics should be changed. Most people thought it should be moved

to about fifteen 'as an initiation into adult committed christianity'. One family reported that their teenage children
thought that confirmation should take place in early adolescence as after fourteen 'people began to be fed up with
religion'. Some suggested that it should take place in the last
year of compulsory schooling. Many commented favourably
on the age of confirmation in the anglican church, but it must
be remembered that some anglicans with experience in religious education feel that there are drawbacks to the sacrament
coming in the middle of the turbulence of adolescence and
that it would come better as an adult commitment to Christ.

The problem of baptism

The traditional practice of infant baptism has been under-
going considerable critical assessment. The problem is especially severe for anglicans in Britain where some two-thirds
of all children are baptised by anglicans but only a small
proportion, less than a sixth, grow up to be Easter communicants. Among Roman catholics the problem differs
only in degree, for less than half of the smaller proportion
baptised by Roman catholics practise their religion in adult
life.

Among continental protestants there has been a debate
about what theological basis, if any, there is for infant baptism
from the new testament and the early church. The position
has been reviewed by a Roman catholic who summarises the
issue as 'infant baptism is still a practice in search of a
theology' (Michael Horley, *Concilium* 4, 3, p 12).

Some of the pastoral issues have been discussed by Nicholas
Lash (*The Newman* 3, 1968, p 136) who stresses that baptism
(and the other liturgical steps in christian initiation) should
be community affairs, which should enable the individual to
declare his belief in the gospel, make a response to it and
involve himself in the christian community by a faith freely
given and freely accepted. He points out that this cannot be
done by the infant. A possible justification may be that the
faith of the relatives will stand instead but only if it is clear
that it will be given to the child later in a climate of belief.

The need for a new approach to christian initiation

Alternatives to infant baptism raise various difficulties. If baptism in infancy is given only to the children of the more devout believers and other children receive some sort of blessing and naming ceremony, the timing of confirmation is a difficulty for it should really follow closely upon baptism or it tends to become a reiteration of that service.

In addition, as Lash points out, teenagers often object that their freedom to accept the gospel has been pre-empted by their baptism in infancy. The only way of meeting this difficulty is by adopting generally some sort of non-sacramental service for all infants, to be followed by a process of preparation extending over the whole of childhood until a solemn profession of faith is freely made. The way would then be clear for baptism, confirmation, first communion and first confession to be entered into over a short period.

There is a serious difficulty about these suggestions for they would deny children any part in the eucharistic community for many years during a period when they are not only capable of taking part effectively in the family meal of God's people, but also when they need this sharing in the eucharist to strengthen their relationships with both God and man. An alternative process would be to continue infant baptism but bring confirmation back much earlier, near to the time of baptism. This would not be so psychologically harmful, provided that some other kind of solemn ceremony could be developed during adolescent years to mark a conscious commitment to Christ; based on free acceptance of the gospel, inner conversion and profession of faith, thus making the adolescent a fully fledged member of the christian community.

To a large extent the liturgical form of the initiation ceremonies, the blessing of infants, baptism, confirmation, first communion and solemn acceptance of adult faith, will depend upon solutions being worked out to the associated pastoral problems and the theological meaning to be expressed in the initiation ceremonies. A few general principles can be laid down, however.

Each of the liturgical rites of initiation should be as fully as possible a *communal* act. They should be incorporated into a weekend parish service, if possible, rather than being private affairs with only a few relatives present. The 1969 Roman catholic revised rite of baptism, for example, is designed for this reason to form part of a eucharistic service. New approaches should be tried out experimentally at the pastoral level, as is being done by many anglicans and in some Roman catholic parishes where first confession is being deferred until after first communion. If the bishops or other church leaders do not encourage continuing experiment along such lines, with assessment of the results, they will not be in a position to give considered leadership upon the problem. There may after all not be any single answer to the problem of the age of baptism and the timing of the other rites of initiation. A lot may depend upon the historical circumstances and the climate of opinion within which the church has to live. This makes it all the more important to have a pastoral assessment of the various alternatives. The real justification of any system will be that it works.

This is a very difficult field from the liturgical point of view because of unresolved pastoral and theological problems but some sort of compromise between the approaches of the baptists and the catholics should be explored by the churches. This could take the form of a ceremony of blessing, naming and acceptance into the community of infants as catechumens, for whose preparation and training as christians the community accepts responsibility. There should then be a flexible approach to the age at which baptism, confirmation and first communion take place, perhaps as early as five or as late as adult life. The decision about the age should be the responsibility of the child and of its parents with emphasis upon a free acceptance of faith by the individual, whatever the age. If entry into the sacraments takes place in childhood, there should be a solemn public acceptance of adult faith later.

If this chapter seems to raise more problems than it settles, it should be remembered that the problems are real ones raised by parents and teachers, people with direct experience of the area concerned. But despite the problems a great deal can be done liturgically with children, and in the next chapter we go on to make some practical suggestions about this.

4

Children and worship

Prayer with children

The family presents an ideal field for introduction to liturgical experience that grows out of the concerns and needs of the participants and is adapted to their situation—something we call 'situation liturgy'. The limits of what can be done are determined by the needs and degree of enthusiasm of the members of the family and are not imposed by rules or regulations. Parents are accustomed in general to having to tailor what they do to the child's capacities and the natural extension of this principle to family worship and prayer provides a valuable element of flexibility. Thus as we saw it is not easy to distinguish between talking about God with the children and actual prayer—the one intermingles with the other. This informality is useful because thinking and praying about God and our relationship with him can become part of everyday life and reflect the child's interests and activities.

Use of discussion in this way is really part of the liturgy of the word. We do not just listen to the word of God, but we have also to understand it and apply it to our lives, for we need to be able to make it part of ourselves. One function of liturgy is to teach, and discussion is known to be one of the most useful ways of learning, provided that it is properly directed.

For children, in particular, this sort of discussion needs to arise spontaneously, either out of a child's question, or when the parent brings something up which catches the child's attention. It would be a mistake to try to do this on too deliberate or regular a basis, eg by trying to incorporate it as a routine into prayers at night. What matters is that it should be a feature of family life, not that it takes place at regulated intervals.

Perhaps we have been obsessed too much in general with the merits of daily or weekly routines and ignored the actual and particular need of the individual or family. While there are advantages in habit, there is also the danger of routine. The habit of always sitting at the same place at table avoids the children having a daily battle over where to sit, and this activity does not suffer from being routine. Prayer, however, can easily become mechanical if it is too much a matter of routine. It can be argued that to go through the motions of prayer, even without meaning it, might lay a basis for discovering a meaning in prayer in later years. There is, indeed, a danger of drifting away from even formal contact with God, but there is a still greater danger that people, the young in particular, will see prayer as only a mechanical observance and the whole of religion—in the way it has been presented to them—as lacking relevance to life. The essential thing is that the child should learn to think about God and relate to him, whether by silent reflection or active creative worship.

There is a place for the child's bedtime prayer, for instance, thanking God for the good things of the day and asking his forgiveness for the wrong things done. But even though one may try to vary the form of this prayer, just because it is done everyday it is unlikely that real conscious involvement will be achieved all the time. It is possible that it would be wiser not to make such prayers a nightly event but to let them take place only two or three times a week, on those evenings when the parents do not feel too worn out, and the children too tired and quarrelsome. Does forcing a child to go through a ritual of formal prayer when he is not in a prayerful frame of mind have any value? There seems to be a danger here that parents may feel they have done their duty if they make the children go through the motions of prayer (even though it has no meaning for them). This is rather like the practice in the past of making young children learn the catechism by heart before they could make their first communion, without necessarily seeing whether or not it made sense to them.

What we should be looking for is quality rather than quantity. We need to enable our children to find in prayer a deepening relationship with God, a real encounter. This does not come with forcing, rather children should feel a need

36

to pray and that is when parents can help them most effectively to develop a prayerful relationship with God. This relationship needs expression that is spontaneous just as is the love that husband and wife show for each other, or as spontaneous as the love of parents for their children. Warmth of feeling and intuitive understanding cannot just be switched on—they need to be given the right conditions to develop but cannot be forced.

One of the advantages of a properly worked out liturgy in the home setting as against 'prayers' is that it provides an occasion and an atmosphere for the right sort of relationship with God to grow. Children are usually far more involved personally in a home Easter vigil or in an *agape*, for example, than in simple night prayers, not only because it is an event that stands out, but also because it involves the whole person —using music, symbol, gesture, dance and visual aids, as well as words.

Where the parents belong to different churches the home provides the setting for valuable ecumenical activity, for the father and mother to work together to develop the religious awareness and response to God of the children. Even where one parent is not a church-goer he or she will often be prepared to join in domestic worship.

The family prayer-meal
These family prayer-meals, sometimes known by the Greek name *agape*, are really an extended form of grace using the family meal as a symbol of the unity and love that Christ called upon us all to show for one another. Briefly, a prayer-meal or fellowship meal includes scripture readings, blessings of food and drink, prayers for the needs of the family, for the local and wider community and the singing of folk hymns and psalms. The 'Our Father' in the Caribbean sung version is very popular with children. The Geoffrey Beaumont version of *Ubi Caritas* 'There is God' (in *Is this your life?*) is particularly suitable too; for instance, the verse 'Let there be no more bitter words and let quarrels stop so that Christ our God may be among us' is very relevant to the needs of children. Modern gospel songs such as Malcolm Stewart's *When he comes back (Gospel Song Book)* are also most useful, for

they help to highlight the outward looking nature of christian living:

> By the light of our living on earth we'll discover his face
> The face of the master is always at hand
> In the face of the stranger, the poor, in the face of a man.

Children can make their own liturgy
Children of all ages enjoy these family prayer-meals; even quite small children, who do not understand what is going on, like the feeling of taking part in what the family is doing and enjoy the candles and the music and eating French bread. Although teenagers may be suspicious of the idea at first, they very often take to this sort of liturgy provided they can have an active share in planning and running it. Even older primary school-age children may sometimes be eager to work out their own prayer-meal themes. Our boys when nine and seven years old decided one week they would like to work out a prayer-meal on a theme of saying 'yes' to God. Pictures were drawn of Adam and Eve saying 'no' at the fall and of Mary saying 'yes' at the annunciation. The elder boy wrote a prayer linking the two events with our own response to God, ending his prayer: 'please help us to say "yes" to God straightaway and do what you ask us.' He chose a scripture reading of the story of Samuel in the temple springing up from bed to say: 'Here I am, Lord.' (This was taken from the *Hosanna* series book on Samuel.) We worked out together new words for the rather overworked (but none-the-less useful) *Kumbaya* tune, 'help us Lord, to love you', 'help us Lord to live at peace', and finally 'help us Lord to be kind, O Lord, to everyone'.

On another occasion, one Sunday, when both parents were unwell and the family was unable to get to mass, we decided to hold a prayer-meal on a theme of 'thank you'. The children dictated a long list of suggestions, with only occasional promptings from the adults, of what they would like to thank God for. The nine-year old checked that the wording would more or less fit in with the rhythm of the 'thank you' song, and even the four-year old girl contributed thanks for the sandpit and for 'colours'.

Among the verses were 'thank you that man can read and

write, thank you for toys and other pastimes', and the final verse ran:

> Thank you for love and laughter,
> Thank you for making man so clever
> Thank you for the whole wide world,
> and for what is in it.

The children remembered the story of the ten lepers and the seven-year old searched the indexes of one or two children's bibles to find it, finally dictating it from memory—sometimes the effort of writing puts children off making their own versions and under these circumstances parents can be used as secretaries! These contributions were then fitted into one of the ordinary prayer-meal forms, leaving out as we went along the prayers not needed.

Children will not always want to take such an active part in working out the form for the prayer-meal but in general they seem to gain a good deal from these forms of family worship. Not only this, but, often unexpectedly, friends and relations seem happy to join in too. Relatives who are members of other churches, particularly of the evangelical tradition, who would be horrified to have anything to do with devotions (especially Roman catholic) of the older type, find themselves at home in services firmly rooted in scripture and in the practices of the early church. One anglican family we know of keeps open house each Sunday evening when all who drop in to share their supper join in the prayer-meal. They say that even those who do not consider themselves to be christians seem glad to join in this form of fellowship and symbol of unity. Parents with teenage children often fear that it would be impossible to introduce such meals into a family with adolescents but it sometimes happens that once the initial reluctance is overcome, the teenagers become enthusiastic and take over the running of the family prayer-meals, bringing their own friends to take part, often from a distance.

Where the older children are concerned, this sort of prayer-meal is probably more acceptable than ceremonies based on the liturgical cycle, but for the younger children it is very important that the feasts and seasons of the church should be brought into their everyday life and made part of their experience in the home. Church ceremonies are not geared to the needs of the children, unless they have been specially worked out for them. Home liturgy, on the other hand, is centred on the needs of the children. Young children in particular learn through seeing and doing rather than through words and they should be given the opportunity to take part in worship that uses actions, symbols, music and visual aids as well as words. The increasingly common use of this sort of worship in primary schools and in the more enlightened parish churches is helpful, but the younger child also needs this experience in the family if he or she is to integrate worship with normal everyday life which is centred on the home.

Feasts and seasons in the home
Easter, not Christmas, should stand out as the climax of the liturgical year. This can be done in the family not only by making Lent a time of preparation for Easter so that children come to look forward eagerly to it, but through decorations, festivities, feasting and home liturgical celebrations. During the weeks before Easter the children will be preparing decorations with a liturgical motif, searching the scriptures for relevant subjects, at the same time as learning to think of others through the Lenten practice of almsgiving. A project can be chosen which captures their imagination— saving towards a tractor in Africa, a well-pump for India, clothes and food for a Peruvian child, or bricks for an organisation aiding the homeless, like 'Shelter'. A visual aid can be made showing the chosen object, eg the tractor or a house for a homeless family, divided up into sections which can be coloured in as the children save the money needed by giving up things like sweets, cakes or lollies. The box into which they put their money will have a place of honour at the centre of the Easter table.

Ash Wednesday and Good Friday can be marked by simple home ceremonies and where the children are too young to go to the parish Easter Vigil parents can organise a short family ceremony with the lighting of the paschal candle, a retelling of the exodus story, and a renewal of the baptismal promises. A detailed account of this and other Easter activities is given in our earlier book, *Liturgy is what we make it.*

It is perhaps the passover meal which is the most effective of all home ceremonies. This is a liturgical meal which recalls the events of the exodus and puts them in their christian perspective. Passages from scripture, litanies, songs, prayers and symbolic actions are interspersed with feasting and laughter. Children love helping to prepare the *seder* dish with its symbolic foods and they themselves have an important part in the ceremony, asking the adults the traditional questions why the night is different from all other nights, and what is the meaning of various foods on the *seder* dish?

Each holy week we ourselves ask in friends and other families, as many as we can fit around our table. Our children look forward to the passover supper for months ahead and we have found that children of all ages enjoy participating; teenagers being most enthusiastic, particularly as they can take a full part in the readings or leading the prayers; and even the younger children, who have only just learnt to read, are eager to take a full part in the readings. We also ask all the children to bring paintings, collages, mobiles or other art forms to illustrate the passover theme, and the adults contribute wine, food or flowers. Before the start of the meal we practise the music, sometimes using a tape or record to give the right note to start with.

Children and the parish

The only difficulty that arises from having such a meal is that the parish liturgy (unless it is unusually good) may well seem rather flat after what is a real communal worship experience. There need not be such a contrast, however, for the passover meal does not have to be confined to homes. For example, one church where the needs of families are very much taken into account holds a parish *hagada* or passover meal in the adjacent hall on Maundy Thursday, before the evening mass. Parishioners, both families and single people, help prepare the hall, decorating it with children's drawings and paintings, setting up the tables and bringing food. Each family brings wine enough for its own needs and some left over in case anyone comes without.

After the traditional blessings of wine and bread and the recounting of the exodus story, the door of the hall is opened as a sign of hospitality and all are invited to the meal. In between the traditional questions and answers all the people sing spirituals such as 'Let my people go' or the modern folk song 'We will sing as we go'. (It goes: 'We will laugh and clap and shout to the Lord who leads us out.') After the meal is finished and the final glasses of wine are blessed and drunk the door is once more opened to show the people's readiness to greet the Lord when he comes again, and a song calling for Christ to come speedily is sung. Then all the people move into the church for the usual Maundy Thursday mass. All the chairs and kneelers have been removed to make more room and the parents are encouraged to let the smallest children come right up near the altar to see what is going on.

In later years this parish passover meal became too overcrowded and a number of families started to hold passover meals in their own homes, all finally meeting in the church for the Maundy Thursday liturgy.

This shows how a parish can provide a service in Holy Week especially suited to the needs of children. With a little imagination and ingenuity the same sort of provision can be made for the other main feasts and seasons. A good way of doing this is to decide a few weeks in advance that there is to be a special afternoon children's eucharist, say on Epiphany, and encourage the parents to help with the preparations and arrange a children's party to follow it. When this was done in one urban Roman catholic parish, the children sat on the floor around a low table as altar with the parents on chairs at the sides. The children had drums and bells and had brought gifts for one another. The priest explained some of the meaning of the feast as the service proceeded, using the question and answer method and simple symbolism like one of the boys bringing up a box of chocolates wrapped in gold-coloured paper. Actual incense and myrrh resin were shown to the children to make the story more vivid. All the gifts and the bread and wine were put together on the altar by children. After the consecration prayer there was another short question-and-answer session about gifts and communion. The consecrated bread and wine were given out, 'See the baby lying in a manger' was sung, the gifts distributed and the party itself began for the eighty or so children.

This particular church is lucky in having people who play the guitar, flute, violin, cello, drum and organ. Normally only one or two instruments would be used except on major feasts. The music for the liturgy each week and for the major feasts is organised by the laity, a number of whom take turns to choose the music, sometimes writing it themselves, and to lead the singing. Further, people are encouraged to try out new ideas about how the liturgy can be celebrated—dramatic readings of the passion narratives, penitential services for adults and children, house masses etc. In Advent parents were asked one year to get their children to paint pictures to illustrate the Advent readings, and the paintings were then used to decorate the side chapel where the crib was set up.

An interesting development here has been the way in which the proportion of the congregation helping to make the liturgy has risen steadily over the years. This leads to widespread participation by old and young and a definite sense of involvement throughout the community.

This parish has found, like many others, how useful folk music can be in making worship mean more to young people. This important development, the wider use of folk music, is considered in detail in chapter 8.

The holding of special masses or eucharistic services for young children in parishes has proved to be a useful development. They are held sometimes in the church itself, sometimes in the church hall with all the children near the table that serves as an altar, the younger ones sitting at ease on rugs on the floor, making the same gestures together with the priest and singing simple folk hymns. Those children who have learned to read take part in reading the prayers and scripture readings, while others bring up bread and wine at the offertory. In some parishes children have their own liturgy of the word separate from that of the adults, and sometimes this is organised by parents who have had training in catechetics.

Another successful form of worship for young people is the

youth vigil, lasting all night, or for an evening, according to the courage and stamina of the organisers and participants. Such vigils have been run in both parishes and schools. Pentecost, with its theme of the new creation and man's response to the coming of the Spirit, is a particularly suitable feast for celebration by young people and a good example of a vigil to prepare for Pentecost has been given by Tony Castle (*Christian Celebration*, Spring 73).

If such a vigil is to have full effect it is essential that the young people themselves take part in devising or adapting the programme. One form of vigil is the consideration of a number of related themes in turn; between these the group goes elsewhere for group discussion or relaxed coffee breaks. Full use should be made of audio-visual media—posters, drama, films, readings from scripture or modern writers, records of folk or pop music with religious themes such as *Bridge over troubled waters* (Simon and Garfunkel) or songs from *Godspell*.

The group eucharist

Often, such functions will not be held in church at all, but in school classrooms or in youth club premises. House masses, too, became fairly widespread in the nineteen-sixties because people realised that they can be a useful means by which many people can come to understand both the community nature of the eucharist and the value of full participation, for instance by taking part in the readings and prayers, or by making up bidding prayers. Where children are concerned, it may often be the first time they have been able to really see and hear properly what is going on and feel they are taking part in something meaningful. Parish family groups are in a good position to organise such masses and also to work out other forms of liturgy which particularly meet the needs of the children or of the parents.

One form of service that is very suitable for family groups to sponsor is a renewal of marriage vows. This can be held on a parish or group basis but is also a fitting ceremony in the family for the parent's wedding anniversary. The children take a full part in this for not only can they make the usual responses to the prayers said by the parents, but one of them

44

can also read the final prayers asking the Lord to help the parents show forth God's love in the family and the world. Such a ceremony enables a child to participate in conscious reflection and prayer concerning the sacrament of marriage, in a situation that has personal meaning for him because it concerns his family life, and helps towards developing an awareness of this form of encounter with Christ.

Other family groups arrange masses or eucharistic services outdoors in gardens or in the country during summer in the setting of a picnic, each family bringing an offering of food for the picnic. This food forms part of the eucharistic offering, that is it provides an expression of our thanks to God for the good things that we enjoy, like food. It is taken up at the offertory with the bread and wine. Children need to be able to rejoice in the Lord and feel the joy of salvation. This sort of liturgy, therefore, which forms part of an outing or party, is an important part of their religious experience. Dance can easily be incorporated into home or open air celebrations, provided at least some of the participants have outgrown their inhibitions and their enthusiasm can act as a catalyst on others. Passover meals often end by dancing round the table, a spontaneous expression of the joy engendered by the celebration.

The liturgical picnic is free to use a variety of forms of expression. At one such picnic in high summer the celebrant, playing a guitar, led an offertory procession of men, women and children of every age, each carrying an offering of food, a picture or some decoration. The people settled down on the grass in a wide horseshoe shape round a low table acting as an altar. After the meditation and scripture readings the community—for the people present already felt they had become this—offered bidding prayers reflecting real problems and tensions of a life of faith lived in a troubled world with an apparently insensitive institutional church. A real sense of community was growing among the participants, many of whom had not met each other before, so that the kiss or handshake of peace had real meaning. At the end of the eucharist the picnic meal was eaten, all sharing out the food they had brought. Many there had stopped going to the ordinary parish mass as they found it a sterile and meaningless experience, but found themselves in touch with the church once more through feeling at home in a worshipping community and seeing that the church is not necessarily identified with its historically determined structures.

Conferences for families

'Family days' and 'family weeks' also provide good opportunities for involving children more fully in worship that is relevant to them. The 'family weeks' or 'days' are conferences where the children are looked after, generally with their own special programme, while the parents and other adults are at lectures, taking part in discussions or having their own liturgy. The *Catholic Peoples' Weeks*, the *Grail* and the Dominican-run Spode House all hold highly popular weeks of this kind, and many family groups or other organisations which recognise the needs of families run one-day conferences in which whole families can take part.

The most effective enterprise is the family week which will usually have its own children's chaplain who will encourage the children to take an active part in the working out of their own liturgy. Their mass can include acting and mime to give point to the liturgy of the word and often they will work out new words to well-known tunes to suit their own needs. Sometimes they will join with the adults at a community mass, often said in the open with the smallest children sitting on the grass round the table that serves as the altar.

Our own children each made their first communion at 'weeks' like these because we felt that the mass there was a better expression of community and provided a more effective encounter with Christ for the young child than is general in the average parish mass. Preferably, of course, first communion should be taken with the parish community but too often this is a community only in name and little or no attempt is made to make the parish first communion mass relevant to the needs of the young child.

The children's mass at one of these family weeks where our younger boy made his first communion took place in a moderately sized common-room, a table serving as an altar. The children stood around in a horseshoe, some sitting on benches, the few adults present standing at the back. The children helped prepare the altar, all joined in the folk singing and at the sermon time a young girl, a trainee teacher, led a little discussion about birthday parties and gave a short talk directed to our boy, likening the mass to a birthday party to which our Lord had especially asked him. At the conclusion of the mass 'Lord of the Dance' was sung and groups of children and adults joined hands and danced their joy in the Lord round the altar. Both children and adults were thoroughly absorbed in the mass and a glow of happiness and joy seemed to go with us for the rest of the day. Certainly the first communicant, generally a rather tough little boy, was radiant for the rest of the day and the following day was to be found eagerly at the top of the communion queue.

Some people find the idea of dancing in the mass rather disturbing and irreverent, but dance has been used in many different cultures and times as liturgical expression and is a very powerful means of communication and expression. Increasing interest is being shown in dance both as liturgical action and as a means of developing religious awareness. This is dealt with more fully in chapter 8.

The family in the ecumenical movement
In the movement towards meeting children's needs in worship another growing point is the ecumenical movement. The churches are coming more and more to worship together, and the problem of separate traditions is often overcome by working out liturgy which does not keep closely to traditional forms but which draws on the common basis of christian belief and life. Such services tend to be worked out primarily for adults but there is also much scope for developing inter-church services for children. Parents in inter-faith marriages, who have been involved in working out their own home worship, should be in a strong position to help in working out ecumenical worship for children for public use. In many ways it should be easier for children than for adults, for the differences in theological emphasis in the churches are not the sort of aspects of christianity that one would want to present to the children, nor are children likely to be so constrained by emotional attachment to denominational customs as adults.

Bringing home to children the reality of a divided world
One very successful example of this was a service for children
entitled 'Us and Them' which formed part of a London suburb's Christian Aid Week project. A marquee was set up on
the local green. There was a market and an auction, a folk
concert and an adult service as well as this children's service
on the Sunday afternoon. An exhibition was arranged, in
which local schools joined, of children's paintings on current
Christian Aid themes and some of these provided the back-
drop behind the altar for the service.

A group of guitarists led the singing of folk songs with
specially written words. The opening song emphasised the
coming together to worship, others were on the themes of
thanks or the needs of the world. The final songs were on the
theme that christian aid is coming to help: 'there are tractors
to help farmers on their way . . . singing hi yi yippee', but the
final hymn was the traditional 'He who would valiant be'.

Early on in the service one of the clergy leaped on to the
trestle platform and got the children to suggest what *we*
needed and had—like doctors or homes and what we enjoy—
like parties and television. The children who had called out
their suggestions were given placards with the words written
on them and stood in a row on one side of the long trestle
platform. After the 'thank you' song the children were asked
about the hungry half of the world, and what it was that *they*
needed but lacked? Other children came up now and stood
on the platform on the other side holding placards, this time
with inscriptions like 'no food', 'no houses', 'no teachers' and
so on. After more singing, a bridge of money was made between the two groups, pennies and sixpences being laid end
to end across the long platform. One seven-year-old became
so caught up in this that he kept on coming back to ask if
he could have more of his saved-up pocket money to give.
Before the final song prayers were offered up by one of the
clergy asking God to help us to aid the hungry more effectively, to show us how to use the good things that we have,
how to build bridges between 'us' and 'them' and asking
God's blessing on all who were deprived of the good things
of life, and asking his blessing on the 'haves' so that we may
be better able to help.

It was not only the children who really involved themselves in the service, most of the adults sang with gusto and clapped in time with the children, and from their remarks afterwards it was clear that the theme of the service had come home to them too.

This particular children's service illustrates the important principle that liturgy needs to be outward-looking. It is not enough to say 'Lord, Lord' and turn our backs on the needs of our neighbours. The emphasis today is on seeing Christ in our neighbour and one of the functions of liturgy should be to help us discover him there. We are more likely to do this the more actively we are involved—not just in joining in set prayers but in making active contributions to the working out of a service and really having to think about what should be said or sung.

A very important part of religious education, and one which has been almost totally neglected, especially in the pre-conciliar Roman church, is this creative approach in worship. Through their experience in home and school worship children learn how to work out prayers and services which are relevant to their own situation and needs. Adults are now becoming more practised at making up extempore bidding prayers but few Romans have reached the high standard evident in many members of other churches. This was brought into relief particularly in ecumenical groups such as those initiated in 1967 by the *People Next Door* campaign of the British Council of Churches, where the ability of many church members, particularly free church members, to make up spontaneous prayers that are both reverent and relevant was most impressive and highlighted Roman inadequacy in this respect.

The place of liturgy in childhood experience
Much can be done too in school; eg many teachers are encouraging children to write new psalms in terms of their own experience and thinking, and one such collection from a London comprehensive school has been published (*Modern Psalms by Boys*, Raymond Hearn (ed) London, 1966). One fourteen-year-old boy wrote:

There is no balance to life without God
God is like the gyrostabiliser in a gyroscope.

Another boy saw God in the image of an orchestral conductor
who also composes life. Whether or not such psalms are used
in worship they represent a field of communication where
education and liturgy overlap.

Both home and school should offer children the experience
and training in creating forms of worship that are relevant
to them. The ability to make up prayers and services should
enrich the child's spiritual life and help him to relate prayer
and christian living. A useful exercise for sixth forms in
Roman catholic schools is to ask the boys or girls to construct
their own versions of the eucharistic prayer (one of the
methods described in chapter 7 can be used). Thus, the young
people come to express why they personally want to thank
and praise God. If we are to transform the world we need to
make sure that our children, who are the christian community of the future, are able to interrelate worship and
action. Either without the other is sterile.

It is most important that children experience liturgy as a
creative activity if they are to understand the 'good news' of
the gospel in a way that is meaningful to them and also come
to understand that liturgy is something dynamic that re-
sponds to the needs of man in his situation. This does not
mean that there is no place for formalised worship that incor-
porates the traditional and historic, but that we need a
multiplicity of approaches. Not only do individuals have
different needs but the same people vary according to their
circumstances and development in what they find most
helpful.

We should, however, be particularly careful about how
much we allow our children to experience liturgy as something boring, irrelevant to their needs and to which they only
go under duress. The average parish liturgy is geared to adult
levels of understanding and we are in serious danger of
alienating our young people if we do not help them to
worship in ways that are meaningful to them.

How effective relevant experience can be is shown by what
happened in one urban anglican parish. Some of the members

of the youth club who had never previously been inside the parish church began to take a full part in parochial life and worship after a youth club holiday on the river where they experienced a simple but meaningful riverbank eucharist with folk music.

An interesting example of getting children to work out their own service was given by one suburban London anglican church which handed over matins one Sunday to a group of 11–15-year-olds, mainly boys. These young people had complained about the boredom and incomprehensibility of much of the usual matins and their Sunday school teacher had responded by asking them what sort of thing they would like to see in a service of worship. They made many suggestions, including greater participation in the service by young people, the use of modern tunes and readings, and no set form of liturgy week by week. The young people were eager to try and work out their own services, although they were warned it would be hard work.

The necessity of getting the service ready for a four-week deadline led to an agreement to compromise here and there, particularly in the wording of the creed. The young people wrote their own confession prayers. New tunes were chosen for some familiar hymns and new words written for some traditional folk tunes. On the day, during the service itself, group members accompanied some of these on guitars and xylophone. One of the girls wrote her own version of the Good Samaritan parable, making the victim a coloured man. The group were also keen on doing a modern acted version of the Prodigal Son and contributed a number of ideas, which were given final shape by the teacher and rehearsed. Quoist's 'Football at night' was chosen in place of the sermon.

In spite of fears that the older generation might stay away from this experimental version of matins a good mixed congregation turned up. To put people in a receptive frame of mind the teacher first played a record of a Babylonian chant, thought to have been in use at the time of Christ for singing psalms. She pointed out to the congregation that we would not find this sort of music acceptable for our worship today, and young people similarly find the usual chants and hymn tunes unacceptable.

The youngest of the group then led the opening prayer and confession:

> Great Father of us all, we are sorry for what we have done wrong and for what we have neglected or forgotten to do. Please forgive us and help us to live more like your example, Jesus Christ. Amen.

After absolution by the vicar, the congregation said the creed together from the stencilled service sheets:

> I trust and believe in God, who cares for us all, and without whom nothing in this world would exist,
> and in Jesus Christ, God in person, who came down to dwell upon this earth to show us the likeness of God,
> and in the Holy Spirit, God within us, through whom we have communion with our fellow Christians all over the world. Amen

and this led into the rest of the service, which was sung, acted, read and prayed with both enthusiasm and reverence.

The general reaction of the congregation afterwards was very favourable and it was a revelation to many of the adults that the youngest members of the church could lead an act of worship in such a reverent and meaningful way.

5

Repentance and conversion in worship

The development of christian thinking about penitence
Conversion, repentance and renewal are the basis of the
christian life. Being united with Christ in his death and resurrection means for Paul (Rom 6 : 5–11) being dead to sin and
alive to God. The mind must be set upon the Spirit according
to which we live, rather than on the flesh and hostile to God
(Rom 8 : 5–8). In the synoptics repentance is the basis for
belief (eg Mk 1 : 15) and we must pray for forgiveness (Lk
11 : 4). For John the sinner belongs to the devil rather than
God (1 Jn 3 : 4–9). Sin is not just a matter of the individual
and God but rather our relations with others (Mt 5 : 23–26,
25 : 41–45), cf also Vatican II, *Liturgy* 110).

Denominational attitudes to repentance, sin and conversion
have varied widely over the centuries. Thus devotional confession was unknown in the early church and those guilty of
serious sin were reprimanded by the leader of the community
or excluded from the company of the saints. By the fourth
century the universal practice was to administer penance once
only in a lifetime after such sins as apostasy or adultery.
Reconciliation followed a long and severe penance but many
occupations were closed to the penitent and he was perma-
nently forbidden marital relations.

During the early middle ages under Irish monastic influ-
ence there evolved less stringent penances after lesser sins
were confessed to the priest as a representative of the community. He would pronounce forgiveness and reconciliation
before the penance was carried out. In the reformed churches
the idea of penance as a sacrament was rejected or, if not,

largely allowed to fall into disuse. A need for penitence was still widely felt, as shown, eg by the evangelical emphasis upon the need for conversion. Among Roman catholics there has been a steep decline since Vatican II in the use of the confessional box and concern, especially among the devout, about what can replace private confession. Sacramental validity is not enough: subjective experience is of the utmost importance.

Karl Rahner has drawn attention to the changes in the fundamental form of penance that are so far-reaching as to be almost incredible to the dogmatic theologian (*Theological Investigations* II, London 1967, 191). Thinking too has changed. Thus the stress in the first centuries was on *atonement*, the long, harsh penances securing forgiveness. Emphasis shifted later to the shame and humiliation of the actual *confessing*, leading to a sort of devotional confession, made often to a lay person (even as late as the sixteenth century) although only the ordained could absolve. Still later the stress shifted to *repentance* (where it is today) and theories of perfect and imperfect contrition developed, a distinction not made in the first thirteen centuries.

The sacrament of penance had its own special liturgy in the early church, including the laying on of hands, but the form has been reduced considerably over the years, the sacrament becoming more an individual, private affair and its relation to the community obscured. Vatican II recognised the need for a new liturgical approach to repentance (*Liturgy* 72).

Originally the devotional confession that is now passing out of use formed part of an earlier movement of renewal, an attempt to bring faith into practical relation with daily life. The trouble is that when it is carried out in a mechanical, slot-machine manner, with many people confessing much the same lists of sins as they did as children, the penitent is not led towards a real conversion of the heart. The reason for devotional confession ought to be to renew the spiritual life, as pointed out by Karl Rahner. ('The meaning of frequent confession of devotion', *Theological Investigations* III, London 1967.) This is its sole justification, for other sacraments can bring grace, and the remission of all but the most serious sins comes through contrition and, above all, the eucharist, 'the sacrament of the living', as opposed to penance, 'the sacrament of the reawakening of the lost life of grace'. According to the Council of Trent minor sins may be confessed, or passed over in silence and atoned for by many other means. Contrary to popular belief and to what used to be said about 'Easter duties' there is no obligation upon Roman catholics to make a confession, yearly or otherwise, unless they are conscious of grave sin, ie of being at enmity with God.

The need for forgiveness

In the centuries before devotional confession was known forgiveness of sin was sought by such means as prayer, good works and fasting. The latter means has fallen largely into disuse but has become a means used more widely by those protesting against injustice in society and this is in line with our increasing consciousness of the social aspects of sin as an evil that denies a full human life to our fellow men. The world needs forgiveness if it is to be brought to Christ.

There are two separate aspects of our redemption. In the past the emphasis has been on sin and the cross. Today we stress the resurrection and joy, but it is important that we do not over-react to the distortions of the past and forget that we are called to repentance, not just once but repeatedly if we are to try to live up to our calling. 'Repentance' translates the new testament term *metanoia* which means a change of heart, rather than just a regret for past sins with little more than a pious aspiration that we will do better in the future. It has been suggested that the word 'repentance' has become debased and it would be better if we avoided it for some time to come, speaking rather of a change of heart. Heggen suggests that conversion means 'henceforth not being captivated first and foremost by one's own need, anxiety and uncertainty, but allowing oneself to be carried along the path on which the Lord has preceded us, so that the messianic event may become a reality in us and so that we may truly be a hand with which God cares for his creation' (*Confession and the service of penance*, London, 1967). We need to work towards the new creation, to a transforming of this world into a community of love. This work can be hindered by too much concern for one's own self-perfection and freedom from guilt. We all know of righteous people who lack the spirit of love and are so hide-bound by rules that they cannot see what a situation demands of them. What is important is sincerity and a sense of one's own weakness, without getting depressed about it. The gospel accounts of Christ's dealings with sinners do not show him dwelling on people's sins but rather telling them to go away and sin no more. He only really condemned those who were smug about their virtues and felt they had no need to change. The parable of the pharisee and the publican is directed to people of this sort. We have to learn to live by the spirit, not the flesh. The christian choice of Christ has constantly to be reaffirmed, much as the marriage vow does not at once achieve the unity of the married partners, but has first to be fulfilled in the way the day-to-day relationship of the husband and wife is lived. We inevitably fall short of the perfection of the sermon on the mount and the beatitudes, but if our lives are orientated towards God our failures will not cut us off from him. If, however, we become obsessed with our own faults and imperfections we will fail to bring Christ's presence into reality in the world. This does not mean that we should not search our consciences and sincerely try to put what is wrong behind us, but we need also to get away from the 'here are we miserable sinners' sort of thinking to realising that we are the risen brothers of Christ charged to bring him to the world around us.

Has the modern world lost its sense of sin?
It will seem to some people that there has been a basic change in the modern approach to sin. The 'permissive society' takes a much more tolerant view than previous generations did of a whole range of moral problems, including homosexuality, teen-age sex and drug-taking. Some people are afraid that christianity has deliberately played down the question of sin in a desire to become acceptable to modern society. This is not true, for all that has been dropped is the previous exaggerated emphasis upon the penitent as an isolated individual, and upon sexual sins. Christians are gaining, in fact, a deeper realisation of the meaning of sin through a renewed consciousness of social and political responsibilities.

All the same, there is a difficulty for the modern christian about sin. The old-fashioned categories, such as mortal or venial sin, have been exposed as highly abstract and artificial concepts that lack meaning in people's actual life-situations. Even the word 'sin' itself has an archaic ring about it. One thinks all too easily of the devil with a forked tail and long horns whose stock-in-trade it is. 'Original sin' too is a difficult expression, not easily understood and all too easily thought of as a sort of supernatural contamination or infection handed on by some sort of magic. It is all very well to explain that it is really a lack of something or a defect in the relationship that ought to exist between man and God but this does not solve the immediate problem of how it is 'sin' in any ordinary sense. 'Original sin' remains as a sort of slogan for traditionalists. It is something that they expect progressives to 'deny' and belief in it is alleged to be a mark of orthodoxy.

We are faced with a situation over our concept of sin that is not unlike the difficulties that we have over our concept of God. The devil with horns as an anthropomorphic figure behind this mysterious force 'sin' has to be rejected in much the same way as the genial old man looking like Karl Marx in a 'heaven' somewhere up there can no longer be regarded as providing us with an adequate understanding of God.

Our attitude to sin, like that to God, has been changed too by our better knowledge of man. Modern psychology has shown how maturity is achieved by working through and canalising our primitive emotions and urges into constructively useful motivation. We now understand that sex is a natural and useful driving force that should provide emotional energy for our spiritual lives. All of this is a process of transforming our approach to sin, for example in analysing 'intention' or exposing the uselessness of a concept such as 'impure thoughts'.

Problems are looked at too often in isolation instead of in relation to the totality of human life and personality. Roman catholics tended to make this mistake in looking, for example, at marriage, as became dramatically clear during the controversies in 1968 over the papal encyclical on birth control, *Humanae Vitae*. Account has to be taken of this need for a total human view at the interpersonal level in the pastoral approach to the problem of sin. It is not enough to replace private devotional confession by a public group confession to God. What God asks is that we make our peace with our brother first.

What is needed is to work out ways in which liturgy can help us to do this. It is no good having aesthetically pleasing worship that declares our own wickedness but does not bring home our failure to understand our social responsibilities. This is true not just of worship but of the whole spiritual life. A glance through some of the discarded devotional books of a previous generation (eg *Garden of the Soul*) will remind one of how much the emphasis used to be put upon sin as an offence against God and upon the world as a potential distraction from God. Love of our neighbour seemed almost to have been forgotten and this should be remembered as a warning to us for this was probably the main weakness in the spiritual life of our immediate forefathers.

In contrast, christians today are trying to work out the meaning of their commitment to Christ much more in terms of social responsibility and a deepening of spiritual life which can follow from reflection upon what it means to be a member of the people of God.

The social dimensions of conscience
Conscience has to become social. This means that to a large extent new ground has to be broken so that we can see the collective and social aspects of our responsibility for failures, which more and more we are coming to realise are failures of the whole community. At the same time, a sense of the personal responsibility of each one of us must not be lost and we should each be able to see our personal vocation more clearly. It is not possible of course to do this in general terms for all the people together. What can be done is to put before people all the varied issues and the considerations that have to be taken into account. By this means each individual is provided with the means to make his own personal assessment of what God is calling upon him to do in the context of the whole social situation.

This means that it is not enough to have, for example, a sermon that reminds people of world poverty, of the dreadful plight of the starving millions and even of how wicked people here are to let their brethren in the developing world go hungry while they live in affluence. We must help people to have a better understanding of personal responsibility. What is needed is a liturgy that enables people to see new ways of relating the teaching of the gospels to the social context of their own daily life. One quite effective way of doing this is by short telling points designed to make people think and give them new insights into the situation. There is nothing original in this, for scripture itself is full of short telling phrases such as: 'By their fruits you shall know them.'

This is the way that liturgy can help form consciences. There is the well-known example in the evangelical discourse in Matthew's gospel (5: 23–25) about the need to leave one's gift at the altar and go first to be reconciled with one's brother. The liturgy comes to a halt until amends have been made. The light of revelation is thrown here on the meaning of conscience and penitence. It is difficult to reconcile this passage, however, with the usual practice of confession, where the emphasis is placed upon making peace with God, whereas the gospel places the emphasis upon making peace with one's brother rather than with God. It is true that there are sins that are offences against God rather than against man. Generally, however, these sorts of sin are not so common a feature in the pattern of modern life as offences against our fellow men.

The gift must be left at the altar and amends made. Confession alone is not what is demanded, but more specifically peace has to be made with one's brother. The aim of penance should be to help us to understand the social aspects of sin and lead us in particular to make appropriate responses to the command to love our neighbour as ourself.

Repentance or conversion and the small group
Services of penitence are one means of developing this understanding of the need to love our neighbour and of the social aspects of sin. They were used on the continent even before Vatican II, for instance in parish churches on the eve of major feasts. They were introduced into Britain in various forms in the late 1960s.

One of the best ways of introducing these services is that

used for the penitential service given later, which was worked out by a parish family group in a series of meetings. The first meeting took the form of a fellowship meal on the theme of penitence, during the course of which there was a discussion about why the sacrament of penance was failing to meet the needs of many people. What was the role of penitence in the life of a christian? What part should communal services play, particularly in emphasising the social aspects of sin?

It was felt that the new services should exist side by side with the older forms of private confession and do something different by providing a social setting favourable to individual repentance, deepening of conversion and commitment and leading to a better understanding of our duties towards others. There are various ways of concluding penitential services, saying a general confession, followed either by a general absolution or a eucharist, or there may be individual confessions, perhaps the following morning if the service is held on a Friday evening.

In the course of the next few meetings a penitential service was drafted, tried out and polished up by this group. The parish priest, who had at first supported the idea, felt unable after all to use it in church on the ground that it was too long (it took twenty minutes) and that he could not skip the daily rosary (poorly attended), but the service was later used successfully by house groups and other parishes.

The success of ventures of this sort shows that penance is not just a personal individual problem and also that it can be tackled successfully at the group and parish levels because repentance is a social matter. It should be possible to devise a series of outline services each having as its theme one particular type of evasion of social responsibility. These could be used effectively in parish missions in place of the customary soul-searching that is too general to be fully effective.

Alternatives to private confession—the role of liturgy
The use of parish penitential services is an important new approach to the problem of penance that takes account of the social aspects of sin. Such services often end with a general absolution, both in parts of the United States and on the

continent of Europe. Private confession is also available for those who prefer.

Another alternative to private confession is to make fuller use of the eucharist. Many people do not think of the eucharist in penitential terms because they have been taught that it is essentially a service of thanksgiving or sacrifice. The eucharist can of course be given a particular emphasis, eg sadness or joy as in a requiem or wedding mass, but it has clear penitential aspects by its very nature. The Lamb of God is to take away the sin of the world: repentance and conversion is closely bound up with the mystery of salvation.

One way of drawing out the penitential aspects of a eucharistic service (or indeed of any other sorts of services) is by group discussion beforehand of the need for repentance and of the nature of our failings. Such preliminary discussions will often provide material for use later in the service itself. For example, a penitential litany may be worked out or the leader of each group in turn may make a brief comment after the gospel so as to provide in effect a sermon of a novel kind.

The discussion beforehand will help to give the service meaning for those taking part. When they just listen to a service people may miss some of the point but after a searching discussion it will mean more to them at a deeper level of understanding. The form that the preliminary discussion takes will depend upon the nature of the service. If the aim is, for example, to develop more fully a sense of sin, this question should be deliberately discussed beforehand. There should be a frank discussion of sin and of actual problems from life and of whether we are lacking in social responsibility for our fellow men. A reading of some item from a newspaper throwing into relief some social problem may be a useful way of starting off such a preliminary discussion but such readings will not usually be so useful in the service itself because they are usually too impersonal, too general and not concrete enough for the particular people in the congregation.

There are two different ways of organising the discussion—either as a five- or ten-minute break for discussion within the service itself or in the form of a rather longer preliminary discussion. If there is a discussion beforehand more time can be given to it, and if preferred the leaders of the groups can make their comments before the service starts.

If the service is for more than about twenty people, they will have to split up into groups for this discussion. The congregation may just be split up randomly as they are sitting but other ways may be better if practicable. For example, people may split up into groups according to their age or the sort of work they do, at an appropriate point in the service, probably where the sermon usually comes. Then house-wives or school teachers, for example, can discuss their problems together, examine the real situation of their working life and bring their thoughts back to the general assembly in the form of a brief point or two outlining the practical problems.

6

Eucharistic worship in different situations

The eucharist has always been seen as the central act of christian worship, and of course we have already touched on it in various ways, directly or by implication, in the previous chapters. In this chapter and the following one we must look more closely at eucharistic liturgy, and at its central thanksgiving prayer in particular, to see how it can become a more effective means of transforming the lives of those who celebrate it together.

The eucharist as a means for building up the body of Christ
The Pauline approach to the eucharist is direct and straightforward. It is because we share the one bread that we break together that we, who are many, are one body (1 Cor 10 : 16–17). For him it is this sharing of the eucharist in the way ordained by the Lord that makes all who believe part of the one body of Christ. The eucharist is a means of growth and renewal as more people come to recognise the presence of the risen Christ and share the broken bread.

Paul has more to say. The eucharist must be done in such a way as to edify the believers (1 Cor 14 : 1–5) and to enable the outsider to say, 'Amen' to the thanksgiving (v 16). One meaning to be given to 'edifying believers' is the way worship provides a means for the cultural expression of christian belief, enabling the church to renew and reinforce its own corporate identity. Worship should also give people creative insight, enabling them to reflect upon their experience and articulate the meaning of their communal existence so as to add a new dimension to their understanding. Thus in the

Agreed Statement on Eucharistic Doctrine ('Windsor Statement') of the Anglican/Roman Catholic International Commission (*One in Christ*, 1972, 69) the importance of the acceptance by the people of the presence of Christ is stressed in order that this presence can achieve its fullest expression.

The effects should be evident. As the Vatican II Constitution says, liturgy is the means by which people *manifest* to others Christ and the nature of the church. The outsider who comes to a eucharist should see in it a representation of the events of salvation, although one of the defects of modern liturgy is that the representation is by no means self-evident to the uninitiated. The full force of the manifestation, however, should come from the effects of the worship upon the nature of the community and upon people's lives; the 'nature of the church' should be such as to resemble Christ. The role of worship is to bring to life the faith that people hold, by bringing them to appreciate new relations between their faith, daily life and past experience. The most effective way of bringing people to understand these new relations is through their active and creative participations in the work of communal self-expression. Liturgical expression can be thus an excellent means of spiritual formation but not if the people just listen to a performance, however expressive and polished. Instead, they must take a constructive part.

It is more, however, than just liturgical participation. When people express the presence of Christ in worship they must mean what they say and live accordingly. An inner conversion is needed. It will be hypocrisy unless the christian assembly, and the whole church, strive to become more like Christ. Thus liturgy should give rise to prophetic witness, by which the world can see Christ through a community of service. A church really like Christ is poor as he was and ready to suffer, even to die like him to bring peace and reconciliation to mankind. Worship should strengthen the community, preparing it if need be for martyrdom, ie to be really like Christ.

Liturgy in its role as a vehicle for creative self-expression should be the means by which the church is able to maintain its spiritual independence against the dehumanising forces of an alien world. This is the way to fulfil the prayer of the

Johannine Christ, that his followers, though *in* the world, 'may be not *of* the world' (17 : 14, 16). Thus, when a christian community succumbs, in particular circumstances, to the forces of evil, as it did in Germany under Hitler's rule, one of the root causes is usually a failure of self-expression. As Carl Amery has shown, this particular failure took the form of a desire to be respectable citizens, more patriotic than the Nazis, and to conform to the ways of thinking of the establishment that then held power (*Capitulation—an analysis of contemporary catholicism*, London, 1967).

A major defence against this sort of disaster befalling the church again can be built up through corporate self-expression of christian faith in liturgy that prevents the church becoming 'worldly'. Such self-expression must be of the sort that would generate a healthy political or social dissent in circumstances like those in Hitler's Germany. More recently, in the 1960s, liturgy played a role of this kind in the United States in the peace movement (see Robert Castle Jr *Litany from the Underground*, in *The Underground Church*, ed M. Boyd, London 1969). So too liturgy can help to preserve the church's independence by preventing christians too easily accepting the *status quo* of the divided world—the comfortable affluent west and the hungry underdeveloped rest.

The eucharistic liturgy can also help build up the body of Christ by enabling the community to present a picture of christian living which any individual can take as a pattern. Even in the relatively short time they spend together the congregation can express common aspirations and relationships, like the first christians who 'had all things in common', devoting themselves to the 'apostles' teaching and fellowship, to the breaking of bread and prayers' (Acts 2 : 44, 41–42). This is a means by which the individual can be helped by the community in his own spiritual understanding and development.

Related to this is the question of renewal. By this is not meant the renewal of liturgy but rather that liturgy should express the needs of renewal within the church and within society. Thus an important aspect of worship is that it should serve the needs of people. The church does not exist to provide liturgy so much as liturgy to provide for the needs of the church. Liturgy has a part to play in relation to all sorts of work done by the christian community, broadening the basis of the work and making it more effective. For example, when christians study together worship can deepen their understanding, or when they try to meet the practical needs of their fellow men, it can show them more clearly what has to be done.

Worship and encounter—the inner life of the body
Liturgy provides the meeting point between the human and the divine. In early Israel the tent of meeting was the forerunner of the temple where the glory of Yahweh dwelt (Ex 40 : 34–35; 1 Kg 8 : 10–13). Christ however entered once and for all into the holy of holies (Heb 9 : 12) so that in the worship of the new covenant 'the ultimate becomes intimate'.

Many people will object, however, that it is all very well to talk in theory in terms like 'the divine breaking through into daily life', but if you come to our church, the priest mumbles the prayers, the choir sings out of tune and the baroque architecture distracts, so that it all seems a pious hope rather than a reality. There is some substance in this objection. Even though the divine is made present there is no guarantee that the liturgy will bring the individual into direct contact with the divine. What it does do, however, is to provide a setting and context in which a two-way encounter *may* take place.

The scriptures are read and meditated upon, the gospel is preached, people are withdrawn for the time being from the ordinary secular world and thrown together with others sharing their beliefs. The prayers should encourage people to reflect upon the gospel and upon their own personal situation as part of the christian community. In periods of deliberate silence the people 'ponder these things in their hearts' as Mary did the message brought to her by the visiting shepherds after the birth of Jesus (Lk 2 : 19).

It is not liturgy itself that makes the encounter. What liturgy does is to prepare the way for it, by providing an organised setting in which man can encounter God. Liturgy itself cannot provide the encounter because it is made up of secular things like words, singing and prayers written by men. There is no question of magic. The purpose of worship is to point beyond itself, ie to take people wherever they are likely to find Christ.

Worship provides, therefore, a basis for the inner life of the body, through an encounter with Christ. For this it draws upon three main sources of material: God and his salvation, which we have learned about from scripture or from the pool of christian communal experience; man and his needs, that is the current situation of those we know or meet, in the context of the command to love our neighbour; and finally our accumulated personal experience derived from our previous relations with our fellow men and our inner reflection upon them. Liturgy can provide a useful service by encouraging interaction and cross-referencing between these three sources of material available for our spiritual lives.

One way it can do this is by setting the context for meditation. Then periods of silence can be very useful. Often, however, the meditative, cross-referencing process will continue when the eucharist is over. This is the real reason (not 'thanksgiving') why people often find it useful to spend time in personal reflection or prayer in church immediately after a service. Whether the reflection is carried out then or later, it should be helpful to use the liturgical setting as the context for a deliberate effort at comparison and cross-referencing, asking ourselves, for example (after Mt 23 has been read), 'In our attitudes to others today, are we guilty of any of the faults of the Scribes and Pharisees?'

Worship, sacrament and ministry

In order to understand the great potential for spiritual development that worship provides, the role of the people and ministers as God's agents has to be considered. The liturgy provides a setting within which Christ acts, baptising or giving communion—his presence within the community should show itself in signs of holiness (Col 3 : 1–17). The celebrating minister acts in the eucharist, on behalf of the people, as the instrument of Christ. Despite this important role of the minister, to refer to him as a 'priest' is liturgically confusing for the only priestly office that he can exercise is that of Christ, not that of the old order now made obsolete (Heb 10 : 1–18). 'Priest' can only have this special meaning in christian worship: the Greek equivalent, *hiereus*, is used more than 140 times in the new testament but never of a christian minister, only of the whole christian people (1 Pet 2 : 9).

It is not the function of liturgy to define the nature of ministry: the first deacons were ordained to serve material, not liturgical, needs. Nevertheless, because the minister takes the role of Christ in the eucharist, there is a temptation to see him as having some magical power passed down through centuries of episcopal laying on of hands, wrongly restricting the spiritual participation of the people.

This distorted view of liturgical action has been refuted, eg by Karl Rahner in an exegesis of 2 Tim 1 : 6 (*Theological Investigations* III, London, 1967, pp 171–176) who shows the imposition of hands at ordination is merely the sacramental outward sign of a continuing encounter by grace between God and man. The minister is placed in a new relationship to Christ and the church and can open his heart to God working in and through him. Hans Küng has shown from new testament exegesis that apostolic succession is an attribute of the whole church—an essential solidarity with the apostles in word, witness and service. (*The Church*, London, 1968, 355–356; *Concilium* IV, 4, 1968, pp 16–19.) Because an active apostolic faith is presupposed, pastoral succession is not given mechanically or automatically by the imposition of hands.

It is this solidarity with the apostolic church that worship must reflect—the eucharist is an expression of the community of believers in Christ. This approach is important in ecumenical work. One of the important achievements of the Anglican-Roman Catholic International Commission in their *Agreed Statement on Eucharistic Doctrine* was to use the Jewish understanding of the passover as a re-enactment as the basis of a consensus view of how the eucharist can be seen as the one perfect redeeming sacrifice. To see the eucharist as related only to a formal hierarchical line corresponds neither with new testament practice nor with church tradition (see Johannes Remmers, *Concilium* IV, 4, 1968, pp 20–27 & Maurice Villain, *ibid*, pp 45–53).

A balanced view of the nature of sacramental action in liturgy should stress the scope for the free action of the Spirit and be based upon the Pauline concept of the mystical body and the diversity of functions within it. Any particular eucharistic assembly possesses the divine power by being part of the mystical body of Christ, in unity of faith with the apostles. The minister exercises that power on their behalf with their consent. Traditionally the minister celebrating says: 'Let us give thanks' and the people give consent by: 'It is right and fitting.' The chain of power thus runs from Christ to the apostles, as representatives of his mystical body, through the local community, as part of that same body and then to the minister acting on their behalf.

It is the community that celebrates the eucharist, not just the minister (St John Chrysostom, Homily on 2 Cor 13 : 3; 61). For St Augustine it is the 'city of God', ie all believers (*City of God* 19, 23). In some eucharistic prayers the Spirit is called down at the consecratory epiclesis 'on and through the community' (John Meyendorff, *Concilium* iv, 3, 1967, pp 27–30). In the modern Roman eucharistic prayer 4 this also is the sense of the epiclesis and also in prayer 3 it is clear that it is the community that celebrates, for this verb is in the plural.

On occasions somebody other than the ordained minister may act as the vehicle of consecratory power; eg 'anybody who has the gift of tongues' (1 Cor 14 : 13 & 16) or 'prophets' (*Didache* x, 7) or, in principle, any lay believer for whom the possibility of a charismatic call must be envisaged (Joseph Duss-von Werdt, 'What can a layman do without a priest?' *Concilium* iv, 4, 1968, pp 54–58).

To say that the sacramental power works through the worshipping community is not to imply that the ordained minister does not have an important role: a heavier burden is actually placed upon him. He has to serve the people, making sure that liturgy becomes communally effective, catalysing human spiritual interaction and making Christ more fully present in and through the community. Not enough preparation for this is given yet in clerical training. Students often work in groups. Not only should these groups be lay ones (not just fellow students) but the student should also learn to lead such groups in liturgical exercises of the type outlined elsewhere in this book so that he finds out how to get the people themselves to create worship, rather than doing the job for them. He will thus see how to make the group an effective part of the mystical body.

Each and every member of the eucharistic assembly must be seen, therefore, as the vehicle of Christ's Spirit, one with the apostolic church, for the time transcendence of 'do this in memory of me' goes beyond mere re-enactment of the past events. The first eucharistic communities looked for the early return of Christ (1 Pet 1 : 4–7) but the death of the apostles brought a painful re-appraisal in which these eucharistic communities took institutional form and wrestled with a variety of pastoral problems. The christians of the third and fourth centuries primarily looked backwards to the institution, so that in the middle ages the eucharist was seen in metaphysical terms rather than as an event giving life to the community.

Only today are we recovering the full sense of the time-transcendence of Christ's presence in his mystical body so that the eucharistic event enables us at one and the same time to sit beside Christ and his disciples in the upper room of the first Easter and also to share something of his future coming in glory. This is the sacramental mystery of worship.

Liturgy must live just as at the last supper
Liturgy can only really live, worship can only truly express joy, sorrow, hope, faith and love if it is firmly rooted in the actual lives and experience of the people who are worshipping. That this simple truth could have been lost sight of is the tragedy of many centuries of liturgical sterility, of remote rites performed in a largely incomprehensible language, idiom and style. It was not always so and now, thank God, situation liturgy has begun to come back into its own. 'Come back', we can say, because this was exactly the description for the last supper itself, on which all eucharistic liturgy, in all its different forms, is based. It will be helpful to look briefly at this creative aspect of the worship of Jesus and his friends.

Jesus and his apostles and friends were celebrating the passover, or *Seder Hagada,* something still done by Jewish households today. It was a domestic affair for a household, for their friends and for any traveller who might be passing by. It was a special meal with prayers and a number of customs and blessings relating it to the exodus tradition. It was not connected with temple worship nor did it involve the levitical priesthood, although it was a sacrificial meal. It would be an informal and friendly type of gathering, presided over by the head of the household or the leader of the group.

It was in this simple, homely, informal domestic situation that christian liturgy came to birth. The disciple John was lying close to the breast of Jesus (Jn 13 : 23). The passover meal is deliberately informal, more so than other Jewish family meals, so that in the rite one of the traditional questions that a child asks is:

> Why is this night different from all other nights? On all other nights we eat and drink either sitting or leaning, but on this night we all recline at table.

Such was the setting for the first christian liturgy.

In case anyone should think for one moment that do-it-yourself liturgy is a new-fangled idea invented by twentieth century radicals, it must be pointed out that there at the last supper the future christians were given their first lesson in creative liturgy on the eve of Calvary by the Son of God himself. The familiar form of the family passover celebration was modified to bring out for the people sitting around the table in the borrowed room the circumstance that this was the last meal that they were to share with Jesus before his betrayal and crucifixion. The old testament exodus was being recalled and within this context an improvisation was made so as to look forward to the new exodus, to the new Israel that was to pass through the desert of doubt and despair, resulting from their leader's death on the cross, to the promised land of the resurrection faith.

What happened? In the gospels and in St Paul we are told that Jesus took bread and blessed it or gave thanks. Very likely this was the usual Jewish blessing, thanking God for the gift of bread:

> Blessed are you, O Lord, king of the universe, for you bring forth bread from the earth.

Normally in the household celebration of the passover the leader would have broken the bread saying:

Blessed are you, O Lord, king of the universe, for you have made us holy with your commandments and commanded us to eat the unleavened bread.

But the situation was different. The passover for the Jews was the annual recalling of the flight from Egypt, a story that was to be retold as a memorial year by year (Ex 12 : 14, 17, 24, 26–27; 13 : 10, 14). But now the final deliverance from the bondage of sin was about to take place. No longer need his followers eat the bread of affliction to remind them of the sufferings of their ancestors in Egypt. Bread, unleavened to remind them of the hasty flight from Egypt, was about to be given a new significance.

When Jesus broke the bread it was the natural thing, therefore, to add to or replace the usual prayer about the unleavened bread of the exodus by the new instruction:

Take this and eat, for this is my body given for you.

Similarly, when the meal was over, the fourth and last cup of wine was drunk, symbolising the prophet Elijah who was expected to return before the messiah came. (Jews still symbolically open the door at this point.) The traditional blessing would be something like:

Blessed are you, Lord, king of the universe, for you create the fruit of the vine.

We are told in the gospels that Jesus gave thanks. What thanks did he give? We do not know, but it might well have been Ps 136, which starts:

Give thanks to the Lord, for he is good,
his love is everlasting . . .

for it is traditionally said after the passover meal.

There was no need however, at the last supper, to look any more for the return either of Elijah, or of the messiah of whom he was to be the herald. Therefore something different was said when the cup was passed, something like:

Take and drink, the cup is my blood
of the new covenant . . .

which referred to what was new in the actual *situation*.

The meaning—for all time

The last supper, thus, was creative liturgy, in which new meaning was put into the traditional household passover. There was more. The Jews are told of the passover:

> In every generation, each individual should regard himself as if he personally had gone forth from Egypt.

At the last supper this injunction took new form as:

> Do this in memory of me.

Where did christian liturgy go from there? In the early church it was straightforward: they assembled, to pray, to give thanks and to break bread, at first openly in their homes, and then in secret under persecution.

Many subsequent developments in the history of liturgy are obviously those that were called for in the conditions in which the christian communities found themselves. For example, the influx of gentile converts, unfamiliar with the Jewish scriptures, would have given rise to a custom of regular reading of scripture, preceding the breaking of bread. And again, as the number of local christian groups multiplied it would have been natural in one of the newer groups for a visiting leader from an older community to open the proceedings with a talk and discussion to explain any difficulties about the new faith.

Once the church had become established from Constantine on, and become institutionalised, it developed set rituals in worship and definite styles of church architecture. The liturgy was much influenced by court ceremonial, and stress was placed on the mystery and remoteness of God. The elaborate rituals performed on remote altars in huge and magnificent buildings were a far cry from friends eating round a table in an upper room.

How is the injunction best fulfilled today? There is no single way—the christian community has grown larger and more diverse. It all depends on the local situation. One thing, however, is clear. A house mass in a neighbour's front room or with people seated around the dining table has a great deal in common with what we know of the last supper. The domestic eucharist or one celebrated by some working group would appear to have at least an *a priori* claim to be the normal descendant of the last supper and a desirable way of representing it.

On the other hand, to suggest, for example, that a sung Latin high mass in St Peter's Basilica is an ordinary recapitulation of what happened at the last supper is like trying to suggest that Queen Victoria's diamond jubilee was really a simple birthday party. There is a connection but it is not at all obvious, and probably rather forced.

What is to be done?

There are two alternatives. The cautious way is to try to relate worship to life by choosing language, themes and prayers that relate to the context and give meaning to the worship. This way presupposes that general principles exist in our liturgical tradition which can readily be applied to any aspect of life. Another, more direct approach is the situational one in which Christ's action at the last supper is seen as providing a pattern for the development of worship. A liturgy is then created out of the actual existing situation that does what Christ asked and what liturgy should do in the context of that situation.

We have already seen a number of examples of how this can be done, especially in the family setting, or where several families from a parish meet together in someone's home. Four further examples now follow of liturgy adapted to particular situations in a wider context, conference settings and youth groups. Other useful examples are to be found in Harry Haas, *Celebrations* (London 1969). Haas, a leading exponent of situation liturgy, has worked especially with people of different cultural backgrounds, Hindu and Buddhist particularly. But we must emphasise again that the point of all these examples is to stimulate readers into working out their own liturgy in their own situation, rather than simply following what others have done. Every situation has its own special features, and no one exactly resembles another.

Adapting worship to the needs of special interest groups

One sort of informal situation that provides a natural opportunity for fitting worship to needs is a conference of christians. It is ridiculous for people to break off, as they often do, and go perhaps to some baroque chapel for a mass determined by the calendar and unrelated to the rest of the day, as if worship had to be kept in a watertight compartment.

As an example of what can be done, at a conference on 'education and the community' the eucharist took place in the same room as the lectures and discussions, scriptural passages appropriate to the conference theme were chosen and bidding prayers were worked out that tried to express in liturgy the morning's work on various views about the social function of education.

Thus a young mother prayed:

Grant Lord that the conscience of the people be moved so that adequate money and energy be allocated to the educationally underprivileged areas.

In the silence that followed the earlier discussion was recalled about the desperate need of families in slums for nursery education, about government that saw education only in economic terms of investment value. How poor an investment slum-area nursery schools are, but how necessary in human terms. Then a girl of about seventeen and still at school prayed:

Lord, help our teachers to show us that religion is something living and not just another lesson. Lord hear us.

Later, at the institution, the words 'Do this in memory of me' took on a deeper meaning. It was not just that people had come together to join in the mass and share the eucharist for this was not strictly true. They had come, in fact, to attend a conference on education. The meaning no longer referred to worship alone: they had come together to carry on some small part of the work of Christ and to make his presence in the world more effective through what they were doing together throughout the conference. All this was included in the meaning of 'do this in memory of me'. Thus at this point in the eucharistic prayer the whole conference was being summed up and expressed in special form through the eucharistic liturgy with its deliberate reference to the command itself.

The integration of liturgy into the conference work was

exemplified after lunch by the speaker referring back to the schoolgirl's bidding prayer—the point that religious instruction would be a waste of time if it was just another lesson—in his analysis of the use to be made of new educational ideas in the religious field.

Similar principles can be applied to a variety of special situations. For example, if scouts and guides are in camp and go on Sunday to a chapel on the camp site to attend eucharist led by a local priest or minister, the effect is rather likely to be as if a helicopter had taken them back for a quick visit to their home church. It is much better to integrate the worship into the life of the camp and the aims of scouting, ie teaching independence, team-work and self-reliance. Thus a clearing in the woods should replace the chapel, vestments are out of place, an altar can be made from logs or rocks (as available on the site) by one team of scouts, while another bakes the bread to be consecrated and yet another works out prayers and reading appropriate to the situation. A camp-fire would be just as symbolic (the pillar of fire or the smoke on Sinai) as the traditional candle, and new words can be fitted to many scouting songs.

Worship for unconventional youth
How can worship be worked out to meet the situation of young people who feel dissatisfied with adult society and react against the 'establishment'? The wrong way to do it is for a group of adults to try and organise a form of worship that tries to make concessions to what they think are the needs of young people. A much better way is to let the young people do it themselves. The idea of doing this sort of thing may at first frighten many adults who have never actually experienced it.

One example will make clear how it can be done and how effective it can be. It took place in 1968 in a house in the outskirts of a large town. There were some forty young people in their teens or very early twenties, two of the latter being seminary students. Most of them were Roman catholics, though not all regular churchgoers. There were only three adults present. One was a friend of the owners of the house, who were away. Her son Michael was there too with his guitar which he played well. The other two adults were a priest and one of the authors (who had been invited because of known interest to come and see what happened).

Fortunately, it was the sort of house where a partition could be folded back to make the two main living rooms into one. Even with this, it was crowded: people were sitting on chairs, on the arms of the chairs and all over the floor. It was not a service in the ordinary sense of the word for there was no set form, let alone rubrics or ritual. It went on for several hours. It started as a heated discussion about the state of the world. What are our responsibilities for the under-developed countries, the under-privileged, the hungry? What can we do to stop wars or the inhuman exploitation of man by man? How sick is our society?

There were a handful of bibles scattered around the room but no set readings. At various points in the discussion someone came up with something that he felt was worth reading. Sometimes it was a passage from a newspaper, sometimes something from scripture like the Sermon on the Mount or the passage from James 5 about the worldliness of the rich.

Out of the discussion came a recognition of our own failings so far to do anything really worthwhile for the under-privileged of the world. Sometimes this was expressed in prayerful fashion, though not in a formalised prayer form. Music was another means of expression. At some point it was natural for everyone to start singing a currently well-known folk hymn like, 'When I needed a neighbour'. On other occasions somebody said to the guitar player, 'Michael, what about that song you made up the other day?' He played and sang it and we joined in the chorus.

Fairly late in the evening when everyone felt that we had got a much clearer picture of where christians stood in relation to these problems a couple of people did their best to draw the lines of the discussion together and ask for God's help to do his work in the world. Someone brought in a loaf of French bread. Someone else poured some wine into two or three glasses. The priest said the words of consecration. We sang the 'Our Father' and the bread was broken as it was passed round to each person, followed by the consecrated wine. After a few minutes silence, a final song was sung, there were leave-takings and people went off home.

If one describes this sort of event to devout christians to whom this sort of thing is unfamiliar, to people for whom religion is a Sunday morning duty of attending a church service or to Roman catholics whose attitude is still basically pre-conciliar, they may well find it rather shocking. But the chances are that had they sat through such a meeting they would have changed their minds. There is no question about it—the event really lived. To see a group of young people of the kind that one would expect to see in a coffee bar or pop music club, but not usually in churches, spending some hours in such a serious and constructive discussion, trying to search for God's will, was an unforgettable experience.

As liturgy it represented a radical approach. By comparison the mass book of the American 'underground church', for example, is much more 'orthodox' in having a basic liturgical structure (*Underground Mass Book* ed McKierney, Baltimore, Maryland, 1969). In the 1960s in Britain, in contrast to the United States, this sort of thing had not really been driven underground. The local Roman catholic priest was not present at the event described but he took a benevolent interest in it and recognised the need to explore new ways of giving dissenting youth a chance to find Christ.

Driving back across the town just after midnight with a number of the young people, they expressed their appreciation. It had been part of their life, an event, but it had given meaning also to the gospel and shown that christianity could be a real force in their lives, instead of just a relic in the establishment world. Interestingly, the only reservations were expressed by one of the seminary students who found it difficult to square up what he had just experienced with what he had been taught in his course about liturgy. He was worried because he felt that there were two views and both of them could not be right. What was he to tell his examiners?

One suspected that this was a rather personal reservation. If there is a criticism to be made it is perhaps on the lines that a group of forty or more people are too large to take decisions as such and follow up the discussion with action as a group. There was, however, within the gathering a dozen or so who worked together regularly as a group who did things and provided a nucleus of informed people able to lead. Very probably, it was the existence of this nucleus group that made the whole thing work so effectively. Here was *situation liturgy* at its best. In fact, it was first of all a situation, and liturgy was allowed to grow naturally out of it without any forcing or artificiality.

This sort of approach is very important indeed because it provides a way back (perhaps for many the only possible way) into the eucharistic community for those who have found the institutional church, and in particular pre-conciliar Roman catholicism, too remote from the modern world and its problems, too authoritarian and seemingly uncaring about human need. We have to get rid of the misconception that it is going against 'tradition' or 'orthodoxy'. As has been shown earlier, christian liturgy originated in and developed through situation liturgy. If anything is a departure from the 'norm' it is the formalised ritual that we had in the recent past that defeated the real purpose of liturgy as enunciated by Vatican II.

It will not be easy to recover the ability to live situation liturgy in the way that no doubt the early church could. The task will require great persistence and creative initiative. If the institutional churches wish to recover their lost sheep, what they have to learn to do is to trust all the groups of people, like these forty odd youngsters, who are prepared to try. The churches must help such groups in any way that they can.

Meeting the needs of an ecumenical community
When a christian community comes together from a number of different denominations it is not easy to see how the eucharist can become their communal expression. This problem arises, for example, when attempts are made to reunite separated churches. In such circumstances people may hesitate to exchange communion with one another because of doubts over validity of ordination of ministers or fear of denying differences in belief. Yet real unity cannot exist unless people become one eucharistic community. This sort of impasse is not peculiar to relations between Roman catholics and others.

A similar situation existed in 1969 and again in 1972 in the attempts to unite the anglican and methodist churches, arising especially over the proposed service of reconciliation.

There are various ways in which worship can help in this sort of situation. One way is to work out a liturgy that is not derived directly from denominational services but which draws upon scriptural sources and tries to find the answer that Christ would give to the current problem. For those, however, who prefer a more cautious approach there is the fellowship meal which looks forward to the eucharist that we ought to be able to share eventually, even if not yet. Thus, the liturgy can either bring people to share the eucharist or, alternatively, prepare them for doing so, while the theologians are still trying to find the answer to this seemingly intractible problem. Liturgy provides a way round the obstacle.

An example of how this can be done, by devising a liturgy that was 'tailor-made' to meet the specific needs of a mixed community was provided during the formation of 'ONE for Christian Renewal' in 1970. This body came into being as a result of a merger of ecumenical and renewal organisations from all the major denominations who pledged themselves to 'accept one another in Christ' and to undertake together the work of renewal. This body rejected all the usual compromises practised at ecumenical conferences and made use of a christian eucharist directly expressing the fact that they were a christian community through their acceptance of one another in Christ.

This liturgy was intended to be christian, rather than denominational. It was worked out from a rough draft by a working party of experimental liturgists of different denominations, by successive trials and revisions of the draft until the final form was developed. It was not put forward as an alternative to denominational worship but merely as appropriate to a special situation in which Christ was seen as primary, and human divisions in the church had become secondary considerations.

The working party had to resolve certain special problems. Thus a psychological difficulty would have arisen if a priest of any one denomination had acted as the celebrant. Therefore, the whole congregation acted in this capacity. This was not because of any objection to ministerial office in the church (there were, in fact, deacons and readers), nor even to the particular role of celebrant but only that it was not expedient to have a single celebrant on this particular occasion.

By this means liturgy was able to give a new expression and impetus to the movement in Britain to make the church one as Christ prayed it should be, 'as the Father and I are one that the world may believe'.

Some three hundred people were arranged in sixteen circles of about eighteen people each round a small table with a deacon or deaconess as leader. This enabled the groups to discuss the scriptural passages which had been printed in full on the service sheets. The arrangement also allowed a closer sense of community than would have been possible in a congregation of this size if treated as a single unit. At the same time the feeling of belonging to a larger whole was not lost.

In the centre of the chapel a table held a large loaf and a jug of wine with sixteen plates and glasses. After the consecration of the loaf of bread by the whole community (not just by the many clergymen present), the deacons came up and broke off a portion of it to take back to their circle. Similarly after the consecration of the wine the deacons came up and poured it into a glass to take back to their circle for communion.

The sixteen circles were linked in three main groups each containing five or six circles. These three groups progressively joined in the prayer from the preface on, which gave a dimension of drama and a crescendo often lacking in traditional liturgy. The groups took sections of the eucharistic prayer, all the groups coming together for the words of institution.

Both folk and traditional hymns were used to guitar accompaniment, the eucharist ending with the singing of 'Lord of the Dance', many of the participants dancing to the refrain as they left the chapel preceded by a drum and tambourine. Someone was spontaneously moved to call, 'Three cheers for the Holy Spirit' and the cheers were raised.

Most people found the eucharist extremely moving. One nun who had been hesitant about taking part was almost moved to tears and for many it was not only an important spiritual experience of unity and peace but also helped to highlight the importance of liturgy as the expression of what the conference was all about. Trevor Beeson writing in *New Christian* (May 28th 1970) said of it, 'the conference will be remembered by many people for a most remarkable eucharist on Sunday morning. There was no presiding minister—everyone present concelebrated; there was a good deal of informality with dancing at the end. And the hoary old intercommunion issue was never on the agenda. A precious vision it was of what Christian worship can and ought to be.'

This eucharistic celebration took place on the Sunday in the middle of the four-day conference. It was decided not to repeat it on the Monday, paradoxically because of its outstanding success. It was felt that it constituted a focal point in the conference and in the development of worship for christians of different denominations. It was enough for it to have taken place just once. It was, then, more important for people to reflect upon its meaning and significance than merely for the same group of three hundred people to repeat it. People accustomed to frequent or even daily communion began to appreciate why some free church congregations share the Lord's supper only at monthly intervals.

At the next triennial conference in 1973 the Sunday eucharist followed the same basic pattern with developments significantly in the direction of encouraging freer movement of the Spirit. A draft eucharistic prayer had been prepared which left scope for spontaneous prayer of intercession and thanksgiving and it was proposed that the morning should start with a lecture followed by group discussion. This was felt to be too formal and a more spontaneous and extended worship was evolved by the community, still using part of the draft eucharist prepared so that people should have prayer to say in common as well as making individual contributions.

Worship started with folk psalms sung at breakfast, followed by talks, scripture readings, reflection and discussions, sometimes in the open air. It included a period of bodily relaxation followed by meditation, and coffee. Finally, children carrying flowers led a procession into the chapel. The chairs had been removed—the people sat on the floor singing and then stood for the eucharistic prayer in which there was a free flow of spontaneous thanksgiving. There was much song, either in common or by individuals who contributed songs they had written and composed. As in 1970 there was no one celebrant, all saying together the words of the institution, and following this the consecrated bread and wine was handed round the gathering, all sharing in the one body. The four-hours long celebration ended with many of the participants joining hands and dancing for joy, singing songs expressing unity and love.

7

'Do this in memory of me'

Adapting the eucharistic prayer to the community situation
For many christians the central eucharistic prayer is the most important part of the liturgy. This prayer of thanks said over the bread of life that christians break and share and over the cup of salvation is as old as the church itself. It is a link not only with the apostles but with Christ for according to the new testament he himself set the general pattern of the eucharist as a giving of thanks, blessing and sharing of the cup and the broken bread to be done specifically as a commemoration of him.

The eucharistic prayers developed in the first few centuries have been treated with great respect, the Roman canon indeed being used practically unchanged by the whole western catholic church for some 1600 years. This was exceptional. The fourth century was an age of great liturgical development but its prayer could hardly be expected to meet people's needs over another sixteen centuries. Normal liturgical evolution was stultified because Latin ceased to be a living language and there was a misguided desire for stability. In the sixteenth century the reformed churches developed their own contemporary vernacular eucharistic prayers but here also revision has often been slow and difficult (as with the attempted 1928 official revision of the anglican *Book of Common Prayer*).

The eucharistic prayer should reflect what the people today, not their remote forebears, feel. Flexibility in the prayer enabling people to express more richly their relationship with God has been rediscovered fairly recently.

Contemporary eucharistic prayers
The use of three additional 'canons' and the change over to

the vernacular in Roman liturgy as a result of Vatican II forced people, especially those taking part in a daily eucharist, to recognise an urgent need for further variety and large numbers of unofficial prayers soon came into use throughout the world. In Britain one of the first examples was composed in 1967 by a curate in a Liverpool parish. It became deservedly popular with many of his colleagues.

It is worth following the development of one new prayer as it illustrates how such things evolve. A Roman catholic prominent in lay apostolate organisations passed on to the authors a copy of a new Dutch eucharistic prayer picked up in a church in Rotterdam, where it was being widely used. It was translated literally into English and tried out privately together with a few clerics and lay people with experience of liturgical work. The prayer drew inspiration from the *kenosis* passage about Christ's humility (Phil 2 : 2–9) and related his suffering to our salvation and suffering in the world today. It was most suited to Holy Week or penitential occasions.

The English was improved and some rearrangements made from the experience of the first try-out. The prayer was then used, at intervals over the next year or two, at a specialist study conference on penitence, for a scripture study working on the crucifixion theme and in Holy Week in conjunction with a christian passover meal. As a result the prayer was progressively modified, removing repetitive phrases and making the language plainer and simpler until it was difficult to trace the relation between the original translation and the final version. Constructive criticisms were sought from the people taking part and these were often helpful.

The need for variety in the eucharistic prayer
It can be seen from the evolution of this prayer how new eucharistic prayers for occasional use were beginning to be worked out by Roman catholics in various parts of Britain during the nineteen-sixties after the council. On the continent of Europe and in the United States an even wider variety was coming into use. Parallel developments took place elsewhere, for example among anglicans over a more extended period. with further revisions of the 1928 version of the *Book of Common Prayer*, especially series II. Although these were official

versions the 1966 report of the Church of England Liturgical Commission makes clear on the first page that its work has been done in such a way 'as to permit the maximum amount of experiment'.

The need for variety was clear to Roman catholics. Once the prayer is said aloud and in the native language of the people, it would be too much to expect people to have the same prayer over and over again, even on Sundays, let alone on weekdays. This is a consideration that forced changes. There is also, however, a deeper factor—the need to bring out more clearly the relation between the recalling of the last supper and the current situation, that is to express in fuller variety the meaning in our life today that the eucharistic act can express, the many aspects of our lives into which Christ enters, in which we 'do this in memory of me'.

The basic pattern of the eucharistic prayer

The traditional basic pattern given below has been used over the centuries in various eucharistic prayers and provides a guideline for study. There is no need for new prayers to adhere to it rigidly and in fact many of the traditional prayers depart from it widely. The reader should analyse the four standard 'canons' of the Roman mass, or the equivalent in his own denomination, to see how many of the elements in this analysis are present.

a. Introductory dialogue. This usually takes place between the leader and the congregation with a traditional christian greeting, a call to prayer and a proposal to 'give thanks', the congregation making known their agreement by some such phrase as 'It is right and fitting'.

b. The preface. Here use is made of the traditional Jewish blessing of God as creator. Praise of God is linked to the salvation events in the life of Christ. Some special theme can be chosen for which people wish to praise God on the particular occasion, ie some special reason for giving thanks. The congregation traditionally respond to this prayer by affirming the glory and holiness of God with 'Holy, holy, holy . . .'.

c. Our own situation. Then some particular theme is taken up from the preface and related to our own situation, eg that

God is the source of all holiness, or how the christian community should show God's goodness to the world. Here there is considerable scope for adaptation to special or local needs.

d. *Prayer for the Spirit to bless the bread and wine (first epiclesis).* A request is made that by the blessing of the Spirit the bread and wine shall become the body and blood of Christ. Here is a chance to express the way in which we see the Spirit working among and through us today to make Christ present.

e. *The institution narrative (recapitulation).* This prayer, although formally addressed to the Father, is in fact, a reminder to all present of the meaning of the eucharist, leading up to the recapitulation of the injunctions of Christ to take and eat ... take and drink ... 'in memory of me'. It is a deliberate link with the upper room and a conscious affirmation of our own unity with the apostolic origins of the church. It is like a summary, deliberately expressing in a sentence or two the meaning of the eucharistic prayer as a whole. The usual Pauline or synoptic gospel form can be replaced, eg by the eucharistic injunctions from Jn 6, or sometimes the recapitulation can be omitted if the prayer as a whole is emphatic enough to make its eucharistic meaning clear.

f. *The prayer of remembering (anamnesis).* The concluding phrase of the institution narrative, normally 'do this in memory of me' (or 'in remembrance of me'), is developed further and given meaning in relation to our own situation. The eucharist is now related to life: we express how God becomes incarnate in our own situation. Here is the focal point. What does the new covenant mean to us? What does it mean to *us* to 'do this' in memory of Christ? Here is a chance to endow the presence of Christ with a fullness and reality, to give an abstract theological concept a concrete, living meaning.

g. *The prayer of service (oblation).* This prayer is also known as the prayer of offering, for the people stand before God offering themselves and the eucharist which they are to share as an expression of their willingness to do God's will, that is to serve him and their fellow men.

h. The call for the spirit (second epiclesis). A request is made for the aid of the Spirit to enable us to become a real eucharistic community and serve God more effectively. In what way do we want the Spirit to help us? What does Christ want from us through the communion we are going to share?

i. Intercession (supplications). Any special requests for those in need or for the good of other parts of the church follow naturally at this point, relating the eucharist to the needs of the christian community and of mankind today. Christ is to be found in the despised, the rejected, misfits and outcasts of our society. We have looked back to the Christ of the upper room on the eve of his passion and now we look out to the hidden face of Christ around us.

j. The final glory (doxology). In conclusion things are to be seen in God's perspective: human salvation and the final fulfilment in glory.

This analysis helps us to see how a group of people working at creative liturgy can set about working out their own eucharistic prayer for some special purpose.

How to construct a eucharistic prayer
The first step is to examine the situation in which the people concerned find themselves, and the nature of the special occasion or need. They may be, for example, a group of people working to help the deprived of a slum neighbourhood or perhaps people who want to express their part in a special occasion, for example, a national demonstration or 'sign in' to draw attention to world poverty.

Once they have made their analysis of the situation they must choose prayer themes for the eucharist that express needs arising from it. They might choose, for example, the need to find Christ in the poor, or to express the unity of mankind in Christ, sharing one another's burden.

The next step is to decide upon where the eucharist leads them in their situation, for example, to the need to share material as well as spiritual goods, daily bread as well as the bread broken in the name of Christ.

They must then work out prayers (bearing in mind to which person of the Trinity they are being addressed) that give meaning to these themes, drawing upon scripture and life to express the full meaning for them and for others. At this point they will have, say, half-a-dozen sheets of paper, each headed with a theme followed by notes of examples. The series should now be related in a logical pattern to the institution narrative under the heads set out in the previous section. They should take care not to force the themes into the mould—not every slot has to be filled on every occasion!

The next step is to decide upon the degree of participation that the group want in their eucharist. This will depend upon various factors, for example the number of people present. For minimal participation the ideas under each heading can be made into a paragraph forming a prayer to be said by the celebrant. If rather more participation is wanted, then each paragraph can be worded a little differently so that the congregation can make a standard response to the celebrant's prayer.

If a fuller degree of participation is wanted the ideas for each theme can be arranged in the form of a litany to be read in turn by readers to each of which the rest make a short response expressing the idea of the theme itself. There is no need for the prayers to be written out; from the notes made each participant in turn can spontaneously pray his or her section of the canon. But it is also effective if some section (such as the communion epiclesis) is written out so that the whole group can say it together; this will be normal with the words of institution, taken from one of the four different scriptural versions of them. The possibilities are endless once a group has worked together enough to feel at ease in creating its eucharistic prayers.

Indeed, once this stage has been reached, free response of the Spirit can be encouraged. It then works surprisingly well to have a free-ranging discussion arising from scripture texts which one or two people choose and read. When it seems appropriate, some bread and a glass of wine are brought in and all who wish are invited in turn to express their feelings by a short prayer of thanksgiving or praise of God. In conclusion, all say together an account of the institution in the usual form and communion follows.

The spontaneous and heartfelt eucharistic prayer that emerges recalls the Pauline picture of early christian worship (1 Cor 14) during which all moved by the Spirit gave thanks. The point made by the apostle, that in the eucharist clear prophetic utterance is more likely to edify the non-believer (vv 16–19), still has its relevance today.

8

The use of drama, prose, poetry, dance and song in worship

If worship is to be adapted effectively to the existing situation in which people live and work, full use has to be made of contemporary cultural material. The role of liturgy is to enable people to reflect upon the gospel and upon their experience in the world, relating them together in such a way as to deepen faith and provide a favourable setting for an encounter with Christ.

Secular prose in worship
This process can start either from the gospel or the world. For example, a preacher may take as his text a verse of scripture like: 'Love your neighbour as yourself' relating it to the secular situation, or he may read instead, eg a passage from a newspaper about objections to the building in the neighbourhood of a proposed hostel for unmarried mothers, ending perhaps with a phrase like 'We don't want those sort of people here', and discuss this in relation to the gospel call.

Not only in the sermon, but elsewhere in worship good use can be made of prose passages of this sort, eg of extracts from newspaper articles highlighting a current problem, or from books dealing with some aspect of man's relation with God and other men, but the passages have to be chosen carefully. In some ways the use of prose is more difficult than that of poetry and song. People do not expect to understand every allusion in poetry and song but are happy to have one or two general ideas conveyed to them. The average member of a congregation expects, however, to be able to understand readily all of a prose passage and his attention is lost once the ideas or language become difficult to grasp.

Prose has a useful place, nevertheless, in communicating an idea or illuminating some aspect of the word of God. Extracts from articles or news items for instance can be used to bring home to people what it feels like to be homeless or how so often the society of which we are a part acts in an unchristlike way. Suitable passages, preferably duplicated, can provide the congregation with material for a practical exercise in analysing the secular situation and working out how a christian should react to the situation. Extracts, too, from classical authors such as Tolstoy or Dostoyevsky or contemporary writers can help people to reflect on the way man relates to man and on what it is that Christ wants us to do. Prose passages are often best used together with other forms of communication; eg one service on the Vietnam war used folk songs about the futility of war, with newspaper pictures of the war projected on to the wall, readings from scripture and from Schlessinger's *Bitter Heritage* together with a talk on the idea of a just war and the psychology of hate. Afterwards those who wished stayed on to discuss what British christians could do about the war. They organised a petition and asked the local member of parliament to come to a subsequent service to justify his support for the Government's pro-American policy.

The use of drama in worship
Drama has a considerable communication potential in worship. Examples range from short excerpts of plays such as *Christ in the Concrete City* by Philip Turner to full length productions of works such as *Jo Jonah*, the folk dramalogue by Colin Hodgetts. Some scripts have been worked out specifically to replace the sermon in the middle of a service, for instance *Standing in the Rain* written for Christian Aid by Brian Frost. This uses a series of dramatic scenes emphasising the problems of a coloured person trying to get a room, or the excuses made by the government officials in affluent countries for not helping the underdeveloped countries. The way drama is used depends upon the time and enthusiasm that is

locally available. It can still be used even if there is little or
no time for rehearsal. Ecumenical holy week services are
worked out annually in one London suburb from the discussion course of the local inter-church house groups. There is
only one week to gather the material and construct the service
which usually includes effective short dialogues, either im-
promptu or previously worked out, which highlight local
issues such as opposition to the opening of a youth club
because of noisy motor cycles or controversy over local education plans.

In one parish drama experience is used in place of the first
part of the mass for those primary school-age children who
wish to join in this activity. Regarding the liturgy of the word
as a means of deepening man's understanding of himself and
his relation to God the drama leader tries to do this on the
child's own level by extending the children's sympathy and
imagination, putting them into situations where they have
to pretend to be other people or things, imagining and acting
out their idea of what it feels like to be such a person or thing
in a given situation.

Bible stories as such are not used but serve as starting
points. For instance the children might act out, in pairs, some
aspect of the prodigal son story, each taking in turns to be
father and son. Themes such as growth, water or light might
be worked on for several weeks on end, developing various
aspects. For instance in the water theme two groups of children were asked to act out digging wells, with one drying up.
They then explored the reactions of the 'haves' and 'have-
nots'. Although it is not possible to measure the effectiveness
of this sort of learning, it would seem more likely to give
children some insight into the problems of the third world
and christian responsibility than exhortatory sermons or
lessons.

Dance, movement and space in worship
Dance and movement are coming to be used more widely.
The Israelites danced often in their worship, and dance and
rhythm have always played an important part in human ex-
perience. There is an account in *Risk*, the World Council of
Churches youth publication, which includes photographs of

the dancing of the 'Our Father' in front of the altar during mass, which opens up interesting possibilities (*Risk*: 'Living: Liturgical style' Geneva 1969).

In one parish at the beginning of the Whitsun mass the children danced the oncoming of the Spirit, symbolised by the rushing and weaving round of red pennants, culminating in the peace brought by the gift of the Spirit. This was danced to a background of relevant scripture readings. They had been worked out previously in the group the children attended while their parents were taking part in the liturgy of the word at the weekly family mass.

In a ceremony for Advent in a London anglican church the congregation were led round the church by a group of dancers and a guitarist, using the 'Kumbaya' theme. At each corner of the church the dancers mimed the words ('someone's praying', 'someone's dancing', etc) with the congregation joining in. After the group had danced the *Magnificat* the people were encouraged to surge on to the sanctuary and kneel there. The group concerned (the Reigate Liturgical Dance Group) also danced a mass in a London Roman catholic church during the 1973 Whitsun festival of new forms of worship. The dance replaced the sermon, expressing the weariness of Gethsemane, the homage of the entry into Jerusalem, the suffering of the crucifixion and the joy of resurrection. Both modern and classical music was used as appropriate. Other groups are also at work using contemporary forms of movement and music—jazz, rock etc.

Congregational participation is one of the main problems of using dance in worship. Sometimes people are so moved they will join in of their own accord, at other times there may be little response. It is, of course, much easier to respond in a space allowing free circulation. The open air eucharist in Trafalgar Square at the end of the 1973 festival provided no seats save the lions and their plinths, so that it was easy for people to join in the dancing that spread like a wave through the gathering at the end of the service.

In our culture it tends to be the young who dance, but they are seldom permitted to do so in official worship. We all need, however, to rediscover and use movement and rhythm if the body as well as the intellect and spirit is to be given its proper place. Killinger in his very interesting book *Leave it to the Spirit* points out that only if God can be felt in the body, in an entire psychosomatic unity, can he be said to have a really efficacious existence in the life of the person.

Given most people's inhibited attitudes to dance in British parishes it would be more acceptable to start with a group performing dances rather than getting the congregation to participate. Kevin Donovan in the Spring 1972 issue of *Christian Celebration* describes a communal baptism in a West London church where teenagers and children from the parish school performed three dances illustrating aspects of baptism; the first dance, to the song 'When Israel was in Egypt's land', symbolised release from the slavery of sin, the second dance was on the theme of the waters of life, and the third accompanied the reading of the prologue of St John's gospel. At the words 'as many as received him' the parents were presented with candles lit from the paschal candle, as a symbol of the light of Christ.

It is often found that those taking part in community worship have no real sense of the others present being there as people. One way to try to overcome this difficulty is to develop worship forms in which the others are encountered as body, not merely as 'spirit'. This is being tried out in parishes as well as by groups of people especially concerned with the problem.

For such work informal surroundings are best with a worship space as free as possible from physical barriers. The first need is to build up confidence and get rid of any embarrassment. The movement leader stresses relaxation of the body and increased sensitivity to the physical and spiritual presence of others.

This new awareness can then be expressed in creative movement against a background of suitable music, eg Stravinsky's *Rite of Spring*. Further progress can be made by developing simple expressive movements to accompany the singing of songs or hymns that are already known.

In the field of liturgy, more meaningful ways can be developed for giving, for example, the 'peace' greeting in the eucharist. More expressive words can be found to go with the simple handshake that is usually given in this greeting to one's fellow christians. Then, when the greeting has become verbally meaningful, appropriate body attitudes can be developed which communicate more effectively the concern and commitment being felt for the person greeted. A simple structured movement, eg to raise a hand slowly and hold it up, may easily develop into an elementary dance ritual.

The value of the expression of feelings through whole body involvement in worship is to engender a real sense of community by experiencing the others present as persons. It can strengthen the concern for others and the resolve to feed the hungry or help those in need, changing the life attitudes of the worshippers. Those who have taken part in it have spoken of feeling a sense of liberation, as though generations-old barriers which should never have been there had been removed. Fears and inhibitions are overcome that previously prevented effective communication and encounter with others.

The growth of a sense of community helps towards the breakdown of inhibitions against expressing ideas and feelings in dance. At an international conference lasting a week the participants were able by the end of their time together to integrate dance with the eucharist, using a folk round dance as a symbol of fellowship, miming 'He's got the whole world in his hands' and moving with linked hands to the 'Lord of the Dance' as the final worshipping activity.

Movement and dance are of course much easier in a large room or hall than in the average church with immovable pews. Many church architects are now designing multipurpose areas which lead to freer movement. Some churches have removed their chairs so that those who want to can stand and move freely near the altar. In one church, where the chairs have been arranged in a horseshoe round the altar, leaving a wide area of space, the congregation are able to move round freely at the kiss of peace greeting their friends.

Poetry in worship
There are three main ways in which poetry can find a place in worship. Sometimes poems are written in the form of prayers and can be used as such in worship. (Examples include Hopkins' *Pied Beauty* which praises God for his creation, and

some of Newman's poems which have become well-known hymns, such as *Lead, kindly light*.)

Other traditional poetry provides material for meditation by bringing home to us the meaning of the salvation events or enabling us to gain a deeper insight into the human situation. Poets whose work can be used in this way include Donne (eg *Riding Westward*), Robert Browning (eg *Easter Day*) and Francis Thompson (eg *Hound of Heaven*). Further examples include Charles Péguy (*Basic Verities*) writing about salvation and the mystery of man's freedom:

> For salvation is of infinite price.
> But what kind of salvation would a
> salvation be that was not free?

and Kahlil Gibran (*The Prophet*):

> Your daily life is your temple and your religion.
> Whenever you enter into it take with you your all.
> Take the plough and the forge . . .
> And take with you all men:
> For in adoration you cannot fly higher than their
> hopes nor humble yourself lower than their
> despair.

This poet has written material suitable for a wide range of themes, including love, marriage, work, death, joy and sorrow, prayer and giving. Underlying it is a deep reflection upon the meaning of the gospel. Poetry of this sort can be used together with prose from classical authors (see eg V. Gollancz, *A year of grace* London, 1950) and classical music. This sort of material will more often be used, of course, in a university setting than in an ordinary parish church.

There will be certain concerns common both to contemporary poetry and to worship, eg concern for the sufferings of our fellow men. It is no accident that poets have contributed much to the actual development of spiritual life and even of liturgical forms. For example, in Holland the Jesuit poet, Huub Oosterhuis, played a leading part in the preparation of the new Roman liturgical texts in Dutch after the Vatican Council.

One contemporary English poet whose work is related to

worship is Joan Brocklesby (*Step into joy*, London 1969). Her poem *Pax* can be used to provide effective dramatic contrast in a service about the need to have concern for our fellow men, share their sufferings and joys. The poem is about the worshipper repelled by human contact who would prefer that the rest of the congregation were not there:

> I shall not go to church again.
> They gave the peace, you see.
> My neighbour put his hands on mine
> And spoke to me. . . .

Another one of her poems, 'Jesus weeps over Jerusalem', can be used to express repentance for our intolerance of others.

> O church, church,
> You that stone the prophets,
> That criticise those that dare to be different,
> That tear to pieces those who would serve you best. . . .

Poems like these (cf also the work of Sydney Carter) are often not prayer in the strict sense. Poetry, however, that expresses concern can be used in worship as a reflection upon the human situation and our relation with God.

Poetry can also reflect the prayer of doubt or of questioning, asking in effect, 'what is the meaning of it all Lord?'. One example is Sydney Carter's 'Bird of Heaven'. This seems to be just as much a valid prayer as one of praise, saying 'Lord you are wonderful'. Even although it is not itself a dialogue, it is likely to provoke a mental dialogue or meditation, an interaction, in the mind of the person who sings or listens to it, between his understanding of the Holy Spirit and of his experience of the world. Poetry, indeed, is often set to music for liturgical use and modern song itself is another important field of growth in worship.

Worship and modern songs
One important role that modern religious songs have is to express the tension between the gospel and the world. The contribution of songwriters to religious thinking has been a remarkable recent development. There is the work of Geoffrey Ainger, Leonard Cohen, Hubert Richards, Malcolm

Stewart, Donald Swann and many others. Sydney Carter, however, is such an outstanding figure that a consideration of his
work alone will give a good indication of the general development.

The importance of the work of Sydney Carter is indicated
by the wide use made of his songs by those involved in
working out contemporary liturgy. He sums up, in an ad-
mirable economy of phrase, the approach to christianity
which sees it rather as a quest for truth and justice than for
absolute answers. 'Present tense' is one of his poems, later set
to music, that epitomises this. 'Holy hearsay' is not sufficient
for man today, it says; he needs

> the good news
> in the present tense ...

Man is searching for the living truth

> I cannot lean upon what used to be ...

We need to get away from excessive dependence on the bible
to show how:

> The Christ you talk about
> Is living now.

This is an idea that Roman catholics in particular need to
think about. In enthusiasm for the biblical renewal scripture
can be used too much, even though the Word of God en-
shrined in the bible is basic to belief. The scriptural form of
the good news is not readily understood by man today. It is
too tied up with the thought forms of an earlier age. It is
important to use not only the actual words of scripture in
services, but also contemporary expressions of aspects of christian life, in song, poetry, prose drama, journalism, art, etc.

The irony in many of Sydney Carter's songs often gets the
point across more effectively than either direct statement or
calling on God to make us more responsive to the needs of
others. For instance, 'Standing in the rain' brings home to us
our failure to live up to our belief:

> We are christian men and women
> always willing, never able.

and the comment on Christ's return:

> In this house he will be welcome
> but we hope he won't be black, Sir.

'The Rat Race' is an outspoken comment on the affluent society:

> The more you have the more you want
> It's time you understood.

It ends up with the poor consumer stealing 'to keep ahead' and ending up in prison. He looks through the bars at the sky only to find:

> A bloody great advertisement
> has blotted out the stars.

These songs are not hymns, in the sense that they do not express corporate praise or adoration, but they do have a place as a solo or group contribution, setting the context for a response to the call of God, which is one of the purposes of liturgy. Some of Carter's songs are suitable for congregational singing, such as 'When I needed a neighbour' which was written for a Christian Aid meeting:

> I was hungry and thirsty, were you there . . .
> . . . the creed and the colour and the name won't matter,
> Were you there?

New verses for this song can easily be made up. Another of his songs that does not use irony and which even those who prefer traditional hymns find moving is 'Judas and Mary'. With its haunting melody it contains the antithesis of the criticism of wasting money on the ointment:

> Oh Mary, Oh Mary
> Oh think of the poor
> This ointment, it could have been sold . . .

with the point that although Christ is going away:

> My body I leave with you still . . .
> the poor of the world, are my body he said . . .

St Peter's denial of Christ is the subject of 'Bitter was the night'. This can be used in services of repentance as it expresses the failures of each one of us.

Carter has a strong sense that christianity is a response to the living spirit that is quenched by the letter of the law. His 'Bird of Heaven' might well be taken as a theme song for renewal. Lock the bird of heaven 'in a cage of gold' or in religion, or in a temple made of marble, but you will find him gone. In the refrain:

> Follow where the bird has gone
> If you want to find him,
> keep on travelling on

emphasises the christian response as the dynamic search for goodness and truth.

The use of 'folk' music in contemporary forms of liturgy is very widespread. The term 'folk' is loosely used to cover the kind of contemporary music and words that comment on the present situation in the kind of language, thought form and melody that has meaning for people today.

Some of the songs that are popular today are traditional—such as those from the West Indies—'Kumbaya' and the Caribbean 'Lord's Prayer', or the French traditional 'Love is come again', while Sydney Carter based his 'Lord of the Dance' on an old tune of the shaker community.

Certain tunes such as 'Blowing in the wind' are used with a number of different versions, often with specifically christian words, such as 'How many times must my people exist, before they know they are one?' Others feel that 'Blowing in the wind' should be used straight in liturgy with its pertinent questioning, 'How many times must the cannon balls fly before they're forever banned ... how many times can a man turn his head pretending he just doesn't see?'

While many songs are widely known there is also a great deal of local creative talent. Sometimes songs express a new dimension in liturgy, such as doubt (which needs to be brought in as it is part of life, particularly for the younger people). Eg 'Faith is hard Lord, in our time, temptation is all around us ... why are there wars, disease and hate? Why won't he stop death? ...' (Stephen Church). Some express social comment as does the following written from the twilight area of Notting Hill:

> Now England is a charitable land . . .
> but we support christianity
> which doesn't affect our prosperity
>> (Geoffrey Ainger, *Dives and Lazarus*)

The same author's *Mary's Child*, 'born in a borrowed room', is based on actual experience.

Other songs pick up the theme of hunger and poverty:

> Let's share our wealth my brother. . . .
> Bingo, bombs and drugs and booze,
> Money to burn and waste and lose for me,
> and a little aid, just a little aid
> (when we can spare it) for you
>> (J. and B. Stringfellow—in *Faith, Folk and Clarity*)

or 'Feed us now' with its catchy tune and pointed comment:

> It's hard for us to listen . . .
> we've got the things we wanted
> we don't want to hear your call . . .

finishing:

> he who doesn't feed his neighbour
> will get no food at all.
>> (Peter Allen in *Faith, Folk and Clarity*)

Some are doctrinal, but speak of events of salvation history in modern idiom. Others show forth the revolutionary nature of christianity, eg Fred Kaan's *Magnificat now*:

> Sing we a song that Mary sang
> Of God at war with human wrong . . .

> We are called on to fight
> with him for what is just and right
> to sing and live Magnificat
> in crowded street and council flat
>> (in *Faith, Folk and Nativity*)

Modern composers and writers are increasingly turning to religious themes for their work, for instance Leonard Bernstein and the creators of *Jesus Christ Superstar*. The combination of drama, dance, music and words in such works gives powerful illumination to certain aspects of the gospel and its relation to life.

Music and worship conferences are becoming a feature of the ecumenical liturgical scene and it is very evident from the material produced there and from the increasing number of songs being published that there is a wealth of creative talent being poured out in the effort to make christianity a living force today. Not all are of equal value but although we need music of high artistic value we also need local efforts, which although they may not be of the highest musical and literary merit do have vitality and meaning for the particular local community.

The folk eucharist
A number of folk settings have been made of the mass and a great variety of folk songs with religious themes are sung, principally at the opening, offertory, communion and conclusion of the mass. Folk music, though not necessarily simple, has a more or less universal appeal. Easily learnt and sung, it encourages people to take an active part in the liturgy. Experience has shown that a well done folk mass will refill the church and usually draw people in from the surrounding areas, so that parishes that do not meet their people's needs in this way risk losing their congregations to those that do. Folk music appeals particularly to the young, but there is no age limit; many older people prefer this type of worship, for them the relevance of the words may appeal more than the style of music.

In the late 1960s for instance, in one outer London parish, the folk mass became the central act of worship for people of all ages. This weekly family folk mass had congregations of over a thousand people, more than a third coming from outside the parish, whereas the other three masses, including one with traditional music, had congregations of under two hundred each. To get a seat at the folk mass people had to arrive ten minutes early. The choir of teenagers and guitarists not only led the congregation in singing but also created their own music. They made their own settings of the mass (*Kyrie*,

Sanctus etc) and wrote words and music for new songs. Even those parishioners who still liked to say their rosary through mass seemed to appreciate music and words in the modern idiom, dropping their rosaries to sing lustily. The total involvement of a parish congregation can be most moving, for instance when a thousand men, women and children sing with great feeling on Easter morning, 'Oh, roll that stone away'.

Most of such a mass is sung. It means much more to children to sing rather than just dialogue the mass, but if they do misbehave there is no heavy atmosphere of disapproval from the surrounding pews of the sort that parents so often have to suffer elsewhere. One mother of a hyperactive mongol child told us that this was the only mass she could find for miles around where she felt that she and her child were accepted. Families are also involved as a unit for they are encouraged to make up bidding prayers and each week a different family is asked to form the offertory procession, small children coming up with their parents clutching the chalice and cruets.

After such a mass people talk and mix freely outside the church or move over to the hall for beer or 'coke' to meet one another. While the teenagers get together with their friends the children play on the grass outside. The feeling of community is strengthened by social as well as liturgical expression.

Starting a folk mass

An important factor in the success of this parish was the high standard of the music and general preparation of readings, prayers etc, together with the active encouragement of the parish priest. Parishes which are setting out to start a folk eucharist should aim at a high standard as a half-hearted attempt with an ill-prepared choir is likely to lead to disillusionment and the abandonment of all efforts to make the liturgy more meaningful. Older children often form a good nucleus for a choir as increasing use of folk music is being made in schools today. It is important, however, that the congregation should not become bored through repeating the same songs over and over again. Once they know a few songs it is time to include new material, and in time one would hope that some of this would be newly written by those organising the folk mass. One largely working class parish church in London has a set of forty folk hymns on which they ring the changes, so that there are always some familiar and some not so familiar songs being sung. Churches which use the folk mass also find the freer and more joyful atmosphere is a good basis for introducing the kiss of peace as a handshake and smile, or communion standing or in the hand.

There are parishes where it is difficult to start such a folk mass because of opposition from the parish clergy. Even then it may be possible to do so by persistence of the kind shown by people in one suburban parish in the South which had little life and a declining mass attendance. A couple of keen women worked together to lobby the clergy and other parishioners for a folk mass. They found that many people had 'written the parish off' and were going elsewhere. After a year or so permission was given grudgingly to try out a folk mass. The two lay enthusiasts found someone capable of leading a folk choir, a guitarist and people to type and duplicate words of folk songs.

Members of the youth club and others were invited to coffee one evening to discuss the project. A choir was formed, comprising four adults, five teenagers and over twenty children. Great emphasis was placed upon high standards. Almost from the start the congregation joined in well.

The result of their efforts was that the size of the congregation and number of communicants increased dramatically. There was some initial opposition by traditionally minded parishioners but this soon died down and the folk choir found that they were in great demand to sing at weddings. The parish priest came to see that the folk mass was meeting a real pastoral need even though it was not to his personal taste. Indirectly, the formation of the folk choir brought new life to the parish and stimulated other activities such as organising concerts in aid of 'Shelter'.

SPECIMEN SERVICES

Introduction

The services that follow provide illustrations of what can be done but are not intended to be any sort of contemporary service-book. They worked in some particular past situation and it may be easier to work on them than start from nothing.

In making use of them you should first consider what your situation is and what you as christians are trying to do here and now. Then assess whether a particular service is a useful means of reflecting upon the situation and helping you go forward. Finally, adapt the service so that it does this more effectively. This task should be carried out by the whole assembly if possible, or by a specially chosen working party. If the work has to be done in advance, explain why and issue the service sheet in advance for approval.

Denominations. The services are not designed specifically for any one denomination. Appropriate changes can easily be made and traditional denominational forms added as desired. Interpret the dramatic form also according to local or denominational custom. Some of the sections labelled *Leader* may be felt more appropriate to a priest-celebrant in certain traditions, while a layman leads in other sections. In small, informal groups people may say nearly everything together but in large assemblies dramatic effect would be lost, and the *leader* sections can then be divided among individuals or said by a single person throughout. A *eucharist* is included in many services as optional. If no priest or minister is available appoint someone to act temporarily as celebrant, or all say his part together, or leave out the eucharist according to custom and local attitude to leadership.

Timing is important: expand or prune the service to fit the time set aside, whether a few minutes or a whole evening. Rehearse while someone times the items. Beware of adding new material to a standard service until it is unmanageably long.

Size. Small groups require informality, sitting at ease and everyone having something to do. Large assemblies require more formality and special measures to ensure participation, eg a nucleus of rehearsed enthusiasts to lead singing and responses. Check that the amplifier works and that readers can be heard. Trial runs with a pilot group can help.

Scripture. Short passages lose context but long ones are difficult to follow unless read as well as heard. Put an important passage on the service sheet, especially if it is to be discussed. Series of short passages should be linked to a theme (eg 'truth' or 'witness'). Psalms 9 to 147 differ in numbering in some versions. The Hebrew numbering is used in this book.

Litanies. This form, in which rhythmic responses are made to short prayers, is particularly useful. If the end of the prayer is not self-evident it must be indicated by a 'key' phrase, as for example:

Key phrase:	*Congregational response:*
. . . we ask your forgiveness.	Lord have mercy on us.
. . . we praise the Lord,	For he is good.
. . . O loving Father,	Help us to do your will.

Service sheets. Type first drafts double-spaced for revision. Duplicate final version single-spaced. Stapling can be avoided by using different coloured paper so that people can take one of each sheet.

1

A renewal of baptismal promises

This is a service that is equally useful for the parish or for a small group. A form of renewal of baptismal promises has been in use now for some years in ordinary Roman catholic parish worship in the restored Easter Vigil. But the service will appeal also to groups, particularly to ones concerned with the renewal of the church and of its mission.

As it is given here, including a eucharist, it could well form either part of a parish mission or provide a 'liturgical evening' for a group. On the other hand, without the eucharistic part, ie omitting sections 13 and 15, the service can be used as the liturgical part of an ordinary group meeting. The form can be used, also, as the prelude to the baptism of a baby or adult, the final song, section 17, then being omitted.

It is most important in the present situation that we should draw upon the resources of baptism as the sacrament of renewal that unites the church in all its diversity.

1 Opening song: 'Go tell everyone' (*in song book of this name*) or 'Love is come again' (in *Faith, Folk and Clarity*).

2 *All:* Remembering the words that you spoke, Lord, to Nicodemus, we look back to our rebirth in the water of baptism and pray that we may continue to be born again also in the Spirit, turning our hearts and minds back once more to God. May this conversion renew your Spirit in the life of the church and in each one of us.

3 *Reader:* Ezek 36 : 24–32 (The baptism of Israel)

4 *All:* Write your law in our hearts, O Lord, and free us from the power of evil, that we may grow daily in our understanding of how we, your people, may serve you in the world, keeping your commandment to love you with

all our heart and our neighbour as ourselves. Put your Spirit in us that we may live and see your kingdom.

5 *Reader:* 1 Pet 2 : 1–10 (A kingdom of priests)

6 *All:* May we become worthy members of that royal priesthood into which we have been admitted by the waters of baptism and consecrated by the oil of salvation.

7 *Reader:* Lk 12 : 49–53 (The fire that must be lit)

8 *All:* May we have the courage to drink the cup that you have drunk, to suffer as you have suffered and to kindle the flame of your justice. May we always strive for freedom, brotherhood and an ordering of society that respects man's God-given dignity, so that all men may become your disciples.

9 *Leader:* Let us recall the promises (that our godparents) made (for us) at our baptism.

Do you turn away from evil. and from all its seductions?

All: We do.

Leader: Do you believe in God the Father, creator of heaven and earth?

All: We do believe.

Leader: Do you believe in the Holy Spirit, the holy catholic church, the communion of saints, the resurrection of the body, and life everlasting?

All: We do believe.

10 *Reader:* Gal 3 : 23–29 (All one in Christ)

11 *All:* Grant that through faith and openness to your Spirit we may make responsible use of the freedom that you have given us and so reach the fullness of christian maturity.

12 Then all say together the following (based on a fragment of an early christian hymn, Eph 5 : 14):

O rise up from the dead
And waken from your sleep,
For Christ shall give you light
Arise, the dawn has come.

The sun of righteousness will shine
With healing in his rays and show

> The glory God gives forth,
> Though darkness shrouds the earth.
>
> O rise up from the dead
> And waken from your sleep,
> To meet the Christ who came
> On earth to make all things new.
>
> O come, be born again,
> The living water flows,
> Receive the gift of life
> And share the peace of Christ.

13 Eucharist.

Leader: Let us lift up our hearts.
All: We have raised them up to the Lord.
Leader: We are gathered together in your name.
All: There I am in your midst.
Leader: Send forth your Spirit.
All: And make all things new.

Leader: Almighty God, our Father in heaven, you have called us to be your servants and made us your children by adoption in the waters of baptism and confirmed us with your Spirit. We join with all our fellow christians, with all those in heaven, and with all the saints of all the ages in giving thanks to you saying, Holy, holy, holy. . . .

> We pray that we your people born again of
>   water and of the Spirit
> May be brought together into one body,
> Whether Jews or Greeks, white or coloured, rich
>   or poor, bound or free,
> That we may serve you worthily as a royal priest-
>   hood.
> Send your Spirit amongst us
> That the bread we offer
> May become his body
> And the wine that we offer his blood,
> Who the night before he suffered
> Took bread and gave you thanks.
> He broke the bread,

Gave it to his disciples and said:
Take this, all of you, and eat it;
This is my body which will be given up for you.
When supper was ended he took the cup.
Again he gave you thanks and praise,
Gave the cup to his disciples, and said:
Take this all of you and drink from it;
This is the cup of my blood,
The blood of the new and everlasting covenant.
It will be shed for you and for all men
So that sins may be forgiven.
Do this in memory of me.

Leader: Let us proclaim the mystery of faith.
All: Christ has died
Christ has risen
Christ will come again.

Leader: May the Spirit that raised Jesus from the dead
Live always with us, your people,
Leading us in the knowledge of your word and
    obedience to it
So that in the end we may obtain everlasting life.
By the gift of this same life-giving Spirit
May we preach the gospel to all the nations,
Working together in peace, unity and under-
    standing
To serve the needs of our fellow men,
That these gifts of bread and wine,
His body and blood,
May express our efforts
To do what your Son told us to do.
We beg you to send your Holy Spirit
Upon the offering of your church,
Uniting all those who receive it,
That the Spirit may strengthen them in truth,
The better to praise and glorify you,
Through Jesus Christ your child
Who lives and reigns for ever and ever.

All: Amen.
14 *Leader:* Let us pray as our Lord himself taught us:
Our Father (said or sung)

All: For yours is the kingdom, the power and the glory for ever and ever.

15 The communion

Leader: Deliver us, we pray you Lord, from every evil, who in baptism has caused us to be born again and our sins forgiven. You who sent us your Spirit of wisdom and understanding, the Spirit of counsel and inward strength, the Spirit of knowledge and true godliness, grant that we may remain yours for ever and daily increase in the Spirit more and more.

(Followed by the kiss of peace and communion according to any standard form)

16 *All:* Come, O Holy Spirit, fill the hearts of your faithful, and light in them the fire of your love. Send us your Spirit that there may be fresh creation, renewing the face of the earth.

17 Concluding song or psalm eg: 'The Lord is my Shepherd', 'Cry out with joy' (Grail psalm cards) or 'God is love'. This is omitted if a baptism is to follow.

2

A renewal of marriage vows

This service presents marriage and the christian family as a figure of Christ, both setting before men an ideal in human relationships and helping married people to live up to it. The solemn human promises that the bridal couple make can only be kept through God who joins them in one flesh. This sacramental recall can be made by a parish conference, family group or single couple on their anniversary. If it is not to be eucharistic, omit sections 6, 7, 9 and 12.

If those taking part include Roman catholics married to other christians, make clear that the promises being renewed are the 'I will' ones, not those the Roman church used to exact about the upbringing of children, and be prepared for memories of acute personal tension associated with the atmosphere in which 'mixed marriages' used to be celebrated. Much good can be done by bringing out such tension and exposing it as coming from denominational differences of human origin, not christian marriage itself.

If engaged couples are present as well as married, let them adapt the text as in 8 by saying, 'On this day we look forward to . . .' (instead of 'remember').

1 *Leader:* The grace of our Lord Jesus Christ, and the love of God, and the fellowship of the Holy Spirit be with you all.
All: And also with you.
The leader may now say a few words if he wishes about the service, for example explaining the role of marriage as an aspect of the christian life, or commenting upon the readings. A small group or single family may have an informal discussion on the theme.

2 *Leader:* We remember the words of the apostle Paul: 'Husbands love your wives as Christ loved the church and gave himself up for her. ... let each one of you love his wife as himself, and every wife respect her husband.' In the sight of God and of the whole church let us sincerely confess our failings in silence.

Lord we have sinned against you.

All: Lord have mercy.

Leader: Lord, show us your mercy,

All: And grant us your salvation.

Leader: Let us pray. O God of Israel be with us (you) who are joined in one flesh; for great is the mercy he has shown to all our families. Lord, may we come to bless you more and more.

3 *Readers:*

Lesson Tob 8 : 5–8 (The wedding prayer of Tobias)

Epistle Eph 5 : 22–33 (Marriage and the love of Christ)

Gospel Mt 19 : 3–6 (Whom God has joined)

4 Renewal of promises

Leader: Will you now renew the promises that you made when you were married?

Couples: We will

(Husbands and wives clasp right hands)

Couples: I have taken you to have and to hold; for better, for worse; for richer for poorer; in sickness and in health; until we are parted by death; and to this I give my solemn promise.

5 Song eg 'As your family, Lord'

6 *Leader:* Blessed are you, Lord God of all creation. This bread which earth has given and families share at their tables will become for us the bread of life. We have received it from your fulness and we offer it to you.

All: Blessed be God for ever.

7 *Leader:*   The Lord be with you.

All: And also with you.

Leader: Let us lift up our hearts.

All: We raise them up to the Lord.

Leader: Let us give thanks to the Lord our God.

8 *Couples:* On this day (anniversary) we remember our being united as husband(s) and wife(wives) and we give

thanks to you, Lord, for all the years we have had together, and ask that we may be granted many more in which we may grow in love of God, of each other, and of our neighbour. We thank you for all the happiness we have had and also for your help in difficult times. We thank (ask) you for the blessing of children remembering that you gave your only Son that we might inherit eternal life. Therefore, we join with all your creation and the holy people that Christ won for you in proclaiming your glory: Holy, holy, holy. . . .

9 The Reader now says the eucharistic prayer (any suitable one, eg Roman 2) up to and including the institution narrative.

Couples: In memory of his death and resurrection in sharing this life-giving bread and this saving cup we offer, Father, the lives that we live together in your service.

10 *Leader:* May all these married people, who share in the body and blood of Christ be helped to cherish each other through good times and bad, to know how to help their children to grow in your love and service.

> O God our Father who taught us
> that love is the fulfilling of the law,
> grant to these your servants
> that, loving one another,
> they may continue in your love throughout their
>   lives
> here on earth and hereafter in heaven.

All:
> Our Father, may we love one another,
> even as Christ loves his church.
> May we live in unity and love
> but let not our love be selfish.
> May it turn outwards from the family
> to our brother, whoever he may be,
> that by our love all men may know
> that we are the disciples of Christ.
> Through him, with him, in him,
> in the unity of the Holy Spirit
> all glory and honour is yours
> almighty Father, for ever and ever.
> Amen.

11 *Leader:* Using the words our Lord himself gave us we sing (say):

All: Our Father

Leader: Deliver us, we pray you, Lord, from every evil.

Couples: May we love and be loved in you, Lord, as long as life shall last.

Leader: Lord, hear our prayer.

Couples: May we understand more deeply what you, Lord, intend marriage to be.

Leader: Lord, hear our prayer.

Couples: May our love, being fruitful in children, continue the work of your creation

Leader: Lord, hear our prayer.

Couples: Help us to bring up our children to know and love you.

Leader: Lord, hear our prayer.

All: For yours is the kingdom, the power and the glory for ever and ever.

12 Communion should be given in both kinds

13 Final Song: eg 'The Lord is my shepherd' (Crimond) 'There is God' (Beaumont), 'Thank you' or 'He's got the whole world in his hands'. (New words fitting the occasion can easily be worked out for these last two, which are respectively in *Faith, Folk and Clarity* and in *Prayer, Praise and Protest*)

3

A service of repentance: a meditation on the need for conversion

The following service of repentance was worked out by a parish family group for use in the parish church during Lent. This service has been used both in house groups and in the Roman catholic parish setting. Congregations sometimes accept it more readily if it is not given a name like 'service of repentance' but presented as a 'holy hour' or 'service of meditation'. For smaller groups use this outline as a starting point from which to work out a new service with relevant prayers, readings and music.

1 *Leader:* We have come together here tonight to try to understand more deeply the meaning of the cross and resurrection in our lives.
   All: Our Father. . . .
2 All sing, eg 'Blowing in the wind' or an adaptation of it.
3 *Reader:* Is 58 : 1–12 (Right and wrong sorts of repentance).
4 The modern problem of penitence and poverty. (This may take the form of a sermon or of a lay reading prepared beforehand by a group. The following example is taken from a reading prepared by a parish group):
   What can we, in our quiet, well-ordered, well-fed suburban parish in one of the wealthiest cities in the world, do to make reparation, to do penance for the sins of past generations—*our* past generations, not other people's, not our neighbour's or our relatives', but ours, yours and

mine? People in the world today are heirs of those sins and live in appalling poverty, in nakedness, in starvation. We have inherited the guilt of those sins. . . . We who live here are morally responsible for the spiritual and bodily welfare of a large number of people living in a stinking slum only twelve hours away . . . how long it takes to fly from London Airport to Lima, Peru, to the parish that we have been privileged to adopt, to offer our help and our prayers to its people, many of them homeless. . . .

5 *All:* Song, 'Feed us now' or 'When I needed a neighbour' (both in *Faith, Folk and Clarity*)

6 A litany.

Leader: Let us turn to Christ asking him to forgive us
All: Forgive us, Lord.
Leader: For being so full of ourselves and our own worries
All: Forgive us, Lord.
Leader: For lack of charity towards those with different views
All: Forgive us, Lord.
Leader: For endangering the lives of others, by such things as our lack of care on the roads
All: Forgive us, Lord.
Leader: For the lack of peace among us.
All: Forgive us, Lord.
Leader: For our weakness and half-measures in trying to bring about your justice
All: Forgive us, Lord.
Leader: For having so much lacked understanding of others and for the distress we cause them
All: Forgive us, Lord.
Leader: For failing to be concerned for the sick, the elderly, the mentally ill, the homeless and all those in need in the locality
All: Forgive us, Lord.
Leader: For our share in racial discrimination, famine and sickness in the world
All: Forgive us, Lord.

Leader: For having lived with so little confidence in the future which you have promised us

All: Forgive us, Lord.

All: We pray together that your kingdom may come among us and that the Lord may grant us forgiveness.

Reader: 1 Jn 1 : 5–2 : 6. (God is light . . . live our lives in the light).

7 Bidding prayers. To be prepared especially for the occasion, for example:

Lord, help us to search out what is your will for us. Teach us not to turn away from the problems of our time but to accept our responsibility as Christians for the well-being of our fellow men.

Guide your people in the centres of learning to find the real solutions to drought, disease and famine and then prompt others to put the theories into practice.

Let our family life reflect the love of the holy family and give us a true reverence for all members of our family of each generation.

Help those of us who have responsibility for young people to guide them wisely so that they may grow to be committed and mature followers of Christ.

Lord, remember those who are worried and anxious. Bring peace of mind to those who are troubled in conscience.

Lord, teach us to search our consciences for failure to live by the spirit of peace, and help us to avoid bad temper, aggressiveness and not trying to see the other person's point of view.

Lord, strengthen the people in our sister parish in Lima so that their great poverty does not lead them to despair. Stir up our consciences to help further so that these people may live a life more fitting to the human dignity you have given men.

Leader: Let us now pray for a while in silence.

8 There are two alternative ways of concluding the service. One is to end with a eucharist, starting with the offertory.

Another way is for people to say 'I confess', followed by a general absolution or individual private confession if desired, and conclude by singing either 'We shall overcome' (*Faith, Folk and Clarity*), 'We will rise and leave the house of God' (*Twenty new mass songs*) or other suitable songs.

4

A penitential service for children

This service is an adaptation of the service for adults immediately previous. It was worked out by a nine-year-old boy
with the help of one of his parents. The child helped to re-
write the words for the *Kumbaya* tune, chose and retold the
bible story, and suggested the sort of things that should go
into the litany. This form is only an example of the sort of
approach. Preferably each family, catechetical group and so
on should work out their own form and words.

1 *Leader:* Let us turn to God and offer him all the good
  things we have done and ask him to forgive us for the
  things we have done wrong.
  Here there is a pause or the children can be helped to
  think up the sort of good and bad things they do.

2 *All:* To tune of 'We shall overcome'

> We have come to praise you
> We have come to thank you
> We have come to say we're sorry
>> O deep in our hearts, we do believe
>> in your love for us, O Lord

> We want to love you
> We want to serve you
> But we find it hard, O Lord
>> O deep in our hearts, we do believe
>> in your love for us, O Lord

3 A passage from scripture, for instance this paraphrase:
  One day in the Jewish temple where people went to pray
  a pharisee came in and looked round to make sure that
  everybody was watching. He thanked God that he was not
  like other men who were bad and sinful and then with his

nose in the air he just walked out of the temple. In came a tax collector—tax collectors often took too much money away from the poor and kept it for themselves—and this tax collector who was really very sorry that he had done wrong just asked God silently to forgive him and asked for help to lead a better life in the future.

And God was more pleased with the tax collector's prayer than the pharisee's.

4 *All:*   Our Father (*sung version*).

5 A Litany

Leader: Let us now ask God to forgive us for the wrong things we have done
For not being kind and helpful

All: Forgive us, Lord.

Leader: For not telling the truth

All: Forgive us, Lord.

Leader: For quarrelling, fighting and teasing

All: Forgive us, Lord.

Leader: For not controlling our tempers

All: Forgive us, Lord.

Leader: For wanting everything for ourselves and not thinking of others

All: Forgive us, Lord.

Leader: For not being kind to people we don't particularly like

All: Forgive us, Lord.

Leader: For not doing what we are told

All: Forgive us, Lord.

Leader: Let us remember that we are all working to bring about the kingdom of God on earth when all people will live with love and friendship for each other. Then there will be no more wrongdoing. One day you will return, O Lord. Help us to serve you and our neighbour with love and do your will on earth.

6 Song, 'When he comes back' (*Gospel Song Book* and *Faith, Folk and Festivity*)

5

An Advent banquet

Christmas is traditionally a time of celebration and rejoicing. The commercial exploitation of the season makes many christians stress the penitential aspects of advent and react by calling for a return to a frugal religious simplicity, much as Cromwell forbade Christmas festivities in puritan England. This reaction is misguided for it is a time to rejoice in the coming of Christ.

Because Advent looks both backwards to the first coming and also forward to the second coming the service is a prayer-meal that looks in both directions. It is a party to celebrate the birth of the promised messiah and also a banquet of hope looking forward to the promised meal at God's table in heaven. Finally, as we live in the uncertain present, it concludes with the eucharist, itself a meal that both recalls the last supper and is also a sign of the future promise. Use this celebration during Advent or even during the Christmas holiday itself for your family, relatives and friends, inviting also someone who is far from his own family, perhaps from overseas.

The meal itself should be such that it can be produced at the appropriate time. Carry out the whole service seated around the table, laid beforehand for the meal, and with candles lit. Rehearse children beforehand with their questions. Use seasonable decorations and have customary Christmas festivities during the meal. Set out bread and wine for the eucharist on one side beforehand. If the eucharist is omitted, end the service with the prayer of thanks after the meal and conclude by singing one or two carols.

1 Preparation.
   Someone lights the candles and all say:
         Thus says the Lord our God
         Who created the heavens and spread them out
         Who gave shape to the earth and what comes
            from it.
         Who gave breath to its people
         And life to all that move on it.

         I, Yahweh have called you to serve the cause of
            right;
         I have taken you by the hand and formed you;
         I have given you as a covenant to the people
         A light to the nations.
         To open the eyes of the blind.
         To free captives from prison.
         And those who live in darkness from the dun-
            geon.
   Leader: And Jesus said to the people;
         'I am the light of the world;
         Anyone who follows me will not be walking in
            the dark;
         He will have the light of life'.
   If children are present one of them may ask:
         Why are we having a party tonight?
   One of his parents or another adult answers:
         We are celebrating the advent of Jesus Christ
            our Lord.
   A second child asks:
         What is advent? What does it mean?
   A parent or adult answers:
   In advent we remember especially that Jesus Christ came
   when our fathers in Israel had been prepared for him,
   and we look forward to his promised return again in glory.
   A carol is sung, for example: 'O come, O come, Emmanuel'.
2 A litany of prophecy (read in turn by those taking part).
   Reader: My servant will be a light to the nations and
            my salvation shall reach to the ends of the earth.
   All: Blessed is he who fulfils the promise.
   This reply is made after each succeeding prophecy.

127

Readers: 'The virgin is with child and will give birth to a son whom she will call Immanuel.

I place the key of the House of David on the shoulder of my servant.

A shoot shall spring forth from the stock of Jesse, a branch from its root.

You Bethlehem, the least of all the clans of Judah, out of you will be born for me the one who is to rule over Israel.

See now, your king comes to you;
He is upright, he is triumphant,
Humble and riding on a donkey.
On a colt the foal of a donkey.

The Lord is like a shepherd feeding his flock.
He shall look for the lost one, bring back the stray.
Bandage the wounded and make the weak strong.

For as the rain and the snow came down from heaven
And return not there but water the earth.
Making it yield and give growth
To provide seed for the sower and bread for eating,
So shall my word be that goes out of my mouth;
It shall not return to me empty,
Without carrying out my will,
Doing that for which it was sent.

When Israel was a child I loved him, and I called my son out of Egypt.

This is the covenant I will make with Israel:
Deep within them I will plant my law,
Writing it on their hearts.

When those days arrive
Then I will be their God,
And they shall be my people.

Know that I am going to send you
Elijah the prophet before my day comes,
That great and terrible day.

It was the stone rejected by the builders
That proved to be the keystone;
See how I lay in Zion
A stone of witness
A precious corner-stone, a foundation stone.

The law will go out from Zion
And the oracle of the Lord from Jerusalem
They will hammer their swords into plough-
shares
Their spears into sickles.
Nation will not lift sword against nation
For there a child is born for us
A son given to us
And the government will be upon his shoulders;
And his name will be called
'Wonder-counsellor, Mighty-God,
Everlasting-Father, Prince-of-peace.'

See my servant will prosper
He shall be lifted up, exalted, rise to great
heights.
As the crowds were appalled on seeing him—
So disfigured did he look
And yet ours were the sufferings he bore
Ours the sorrows he carried.
By his sufferings shall my servant justify many,
Taking their faults on himself.
Harshly dealt with he bore it humbly.
He never opened his mouth,
Like a lamb that is led to the slaughter-house.

I have endowed him with my spirit
That he may bring true justice to the nations.
He does not break the crushed reed
Nor quench the wavering flame.
He will not fail or be discouraged
Until true justice is established on the earth.

I gazed into the visions of the night
And I saw, coming on the clouds of heaven,
One like a son of man.
His dominion shall not pass away
And his kingdom shall not be destroyed.

For the day is coming now, burning like a furnace;
When all the arrogant and all evil-doers will be stubble;
The day that comes shall burn them up.
But for you who fear my name,
The sun of righteousness shall shine out,
with healing in his rays.

A voice cries, 'Prepare in the wilderness
A way for the Lord
Make a straight highway for our God
Across the desert.'
Let every valley be filled in,
Every mountain and hill laid low.
Then the glory of the Lord shall be revealed
And all mankind shall see it.

3 A litany of repentance (The readers should pause after each response)
Leader: Our fathers were asked to do penance in the desert to prepare for your coming on earth, O Lord. Help us, your faithful people, to turn back to God so that we may meet the light of your day.
Reader: Are our hearts and minds open to you, Lord?
All: Help us to be ready for your coming.

Reader: When can your will be done on earth as it is in heaven?

All: Help us to be ready for your coming.

Reader: How much of our lives have we kept from you, O Lord?

All: Help us to be ready for your coming.

Reader: Will we give up what we were doing when something else is needed?

All: Help us to be ready for your coming.

Reader: Have we understood what the word was made flesh means if we cannot see Christ in our fellow men?

All: Help us to be ready for your coming.

Reader: Have we done enough to bring about your kingdom on earth?

All: Help us to be ready for your coming.

Reader: Have we lived as if we really expected you to return?

All: Help us to be ready for your coming.

Reader: Are we prepared to remake the world in your image or do we like it better as it is?

All: Help us to be ready for your coming.

Reader: Have we used the gifts you have given us to build up the body of Christ to its fullness?

All: Help us to be ready for your coming.

Reader: Have we forgotten that your church must be like a pilgrim in a foreign land?

All: Help us to be ready for your coming.

Reader: Do we really want your eternal life more than the things of this world?

All: Help us to be ready for your coming.

Reader: You, Lord, are the living bread which has come down from heaven, your flesh given for the life of the world.

All: Come Lord, do not delay.

Reader: The grass withers, the flower falls but your word remains for ever.

All: Come Lord, do not delay.

Reader: We are your people and you are our God.

All: Come Lord, do not delay.

Reader: You gave yourself for the sins of many and we wait for the fullness of your salvation.

All: Come Lord, do not delay.

Reader: Put your law in our minds and write it on our hearts.

All: Come Lord, do not delay.

Reader: The day of the Lord will be a day of judgement.

All: Come Lord, do not delay.

Reader: The lion will lie down with the lamb and man will not kill man any more.

All: Come Lord, do not delay.

Reader: In the new heaven and the new earth righteousness will abound.

All: Come Lord, do not delay.

Reader: O grave where is your victory, O death where is your sting?

All: Come Lord, do not delay.

Reader: Your day will be entirely a holy day.

All: Come Lord, do not delay.

5 The shared meal. The leader now takes any single items of food and drink from the table in front of him as he says the blessing.

Leader: Blessed are you, O Lord, our God, creator of this food and drink that we share together as a sign of your kingdom, which is to come in glory, and yet is already here now in so far as you live among us in the love that we have for one another.

At this point the meal is eaten

6 The eucharist. At the end of the meal all say:

We thank you, O Lord our God, by whose goodness we have shared this meal together. We recall that when the messiah came to fulfil your promises he shared such a meal with his friends. As we know him in the bread that we are to break we look forward to the banquet that you have prepared for us at your heavenly table and we proclaim the glory of your salvation by singing (saying):

Holy, holy, holy, . . .

Leader: In your day you sent the saviour
to take flesh as your Son,
born of the Spirit and of the virgin.

He came to those who believed in you
to make them your holy people
and to deliver them from suffering

Send now your Spirit into this place
that we gathered together here in his name
may be united with him and with all the saints
by sharing his body and blood
in truth, faith and love.

We recall that he, on the night before he suf-
fered,
making known his resurrection to men,
took bread and gave you thanks.
He broke the bread,
gave it to his disciples and said:
'Take this, all of you, and eat it:
This is my body which will be given up for you'
When supper was ended, he took the cup.
Again he gave you thanks and praise
gave the cup to his disciples and said:
'Take this, all of you, and drink from it:
This is the cup of my blood,
the blood of the new and everlasting covenant.
It will be shed for you and for all men
so that sins may be forgiven.
Do this in memory of me.'

All: In this season we remember, therefore,
the coming of the saviour in the dawn of your
day
and that the Baptist called upon us to do penance
and prepare a path for him.
May the bread we break
and the cup we share
help us to do this
and make him live among us.

Leader: We look for the return of the Son of Man
In the daylight of your glory;
for the fullness of our deliverance
and for our bodies to be set free
so that we may be united with Jesus Christ
and all the saints of all the ages,
in the home he has prepared for us.

All: Christ has come!
May he make all things new!
May we see your day!
Come Lord, do not delay!

Leader: Therefore, looking for the coming of your kingdom, we sing:

All: Our Father

Leader: We have come together in your name.

All: May we be together in your kingdom!
Lamb of God, you take away the sins of the world, have mercy on us.
Lamb of God, you take away the sins of the world, have mercy on us.
Lamb of God, you take away the sins of the world, grant us peace.

At this point the kiss of peace can be given (as desired, embrace or handshake) starting from the leader round the table, each person saying to the next: 'Peace be with you.'

Then communion is given in both kinds round the table each person saying in turn to his neighbour: 'The body of Christ' and 'The blood of Christ.'

7 Final song, eg 'Standing in the rain' (*Faith, Folk and Nativity*)

6

The real meaning of Christmas

In contrast with the Advent banquet this is a service in which the implications of the incarnation are considered in a world full of violence, poverty, racialism, hunger, and indifference to the needs of fellow human beings.

Hold the service in a hall for the parish or ecumenically, for a number of parishes, Alternatively use it for a special group such as youth, or let a group (eg 'Family' or 'War on Want' group) hold it in a home, asking in as many interested people as there is room for. Get a small group to rehearse the music which may be unfamiliar. 'Standing in the Rain' can be sung as a solo with everyone joining in the chorus.

 1 Opening song: 'Mary's child' (in *Faith, Folk and Nativity*).
 2 Readings.
 Reader: A prophecy of the coming messiah:
 Here is my servant whom I uphold . . . (Is 42 : 1–4)
 Reader: As John the apostle tells us;
      'The word was made flesh,'
      but what has the world made of his justice?
      'He was in the world
      that had its being through him,
      and the world did not know him.
      He came to his own domain
      and his own people did not accept him.'
One Christmas the folk singer Joan Baez was sent to prison for demonstrating against the Vietnam war. When reporters wanted to know how she liked going to prison for Christmas, she asked, 'Is this not what Christmas is really about?' What do we think it is about?
 Reader: Reads from a newspaper an account of Christmas shopping or other commercial activity.

Reader: 'Feed my little ones' (C. Day Lewis, written for Oxfam).
How many children starving, did you say?
A million? Five million? It is sad. . . .
Or some similar poem can be read.
Song: 'Magnificat now' (*Faith, Folk and Nativity*) or 'Feed us now, O Son of God' (*Faith, Folk and Clarity*) or other folk song.
Reader: At Bethlehem 'there was no room at the inn'. In any of our large cities there are thousands of homeless families. It is a terrible thing that even in our affluent society in Britain we have thousands of families without proper homes, living in conditions of overcrowding and squalor; in rooms over-run with rats or damp streaming down the walls and sewage rising up out over the pan and seeping through the ceilings. People living in conditions like this, however, are lucky compared to those families which have been broken up, through no fault of their own, because they can find nowhere to live together. Our hearts are touched by 'Shelter' advertisements, we find a few shillings for this or other housing aid societies but are we doing enough? Are we loving our neighbour as ourselves when we tolerate families being broken up or living in sub-human conditions?
(Alternatively something from a newspaper should be read.)
Reader: Mt 25 : 31–46. (For I was hungry and you gave me food . . .)

Reader:	A suitable poem, such as Huub Oosterhuis gives on pp 74–6 of *Prayers, Poems and Songs*.
All:	A song, eg 'When I needed a neighbour' (*Faith, Folk and Clarity*).

3 Litany.

Reader:	People celebrate Christmas, which is your coming, by over-eating and drinking too much; but the Baptist did it by calling for penance and living on locusts and wild honey.
All:	Help us to see what Christmas means.
Reader:	Will the voice crying in the wilderness be heard at the office parties and in the crowded department stores?

All: Help us to see what Christmas means.
Reader: Parcels for the pensioners on Christmas Eve but did you really want goodwill to end on Boxing Day?
All: Help us to see what Christmas means.
Reader: Is it the season of turkeys, gifts and parties or is it the birthday of love?
All: Help us to see what Christmas means.
Reader: If you come to the outcasts and sinners, did you not come also to the homeless, the unmarried mothers and the drug addicts?
All: Help us to see what Christmas means.
Reader: If Christ is to be found in people are they not more important than outdated rules, laws, social systems and our own economic needs?
All: Help us to see what Christmas means.
Reader: How near do we want you to be—two thousand years ago in Bethlehem, or in our suffering neighbour?
All: Help us to see what Christmas means.
Reader: The word was made flesh, but was the skin only white?
All: Help us to see what Christmas means.
Reader: The word was made flesh and man burns that flesh with napalm.
All: Help us to see what Christmas means.
Reader: Israel only gave you a stable for your birth but today the world cannot provide even this luxury for many of its children to be born.
All: Help us to see what Christmas means.

4 A simple meal of bread and cheese is now eaten. It is either handed round or collected from a side table. Either just before, or while this is being done, either a reader or all say:

Half the world are hungry—heaven cries for justice,
Faster than sound we fly and even walk the moon's face.
Can we not feed the poor and end the need among us?
Bread of life we break, 'Do this for me', said Jesus,
'You must love each other just as I have loved you'.

137

When we take the body of Christ, let's think this thing
  through,
What can it really mean to share it with each other
And fail to divide the food of the earth with our brother?

During the meal there can be an informal discussion of
the issues raised. Material can be distributed outlining
practical steps that can be taken. (This can be obtained
from Christian Aid, Oxfam, Shelter etc.) At the end of
the meal the leader calls for a collection:

After the collection someone (if possible an African or
Asian) reads:

What you give helps to relieve famine among us (people)
in Africa and Asia but even more than your charity, we
(they) ask for a just share of the world's resources, for a
trade and political system that is fair. We (they), the poor
of the world do not just want the left-overs from you the
rich but rather to be accepted as your brothers to play a
full part in shaping the future of the world. We (they)
who so recently lived under colonial rule do not ask just
for the freedom that has been given but rather for the
opportunity for full human development. We (they) ask
for these things in the name of Christ as men and women
created in the image of God.

5 Concluding song: 'Come, O come Emmanuel' (or other
suitable song or carol).

7

A Good Friday service for young children

The children (or parents if the children are not old enough) build a tomb in the garden with large stones. If possible set it in a place with plenty of spring flowers to form a suitable surround for the empty tomb of the resurrection which the model will become on Easter morning. Meanwhile a simple cross made out of two bits of wood is placed nearby.

One of the children places a figure of Christ in the tomb (this can be a picture drawn by one of the children or a figure from a crucifix). Another child places a large stone against the opening. Either during this or afterwards the following reproaches are said or sung.

Leader: O my people, what have I done to you or how have I grieved you?
Answer me.

All: Because I led you out of Egypt you have prepared a cross for your saviour, who has come to bring you new life.

A further five or six reproaches should be taken from the Good Friday liturgy, where possible simplifying the language.

Song: 'Dust, Dust and Ashes' (*Prayer, Praise and Protest*).

All: Lord, you gave up your life for your people, to bring us out of darkness into the light back to your Father. Help us to try hard to do what pleases you, when we remember how much you have done for us. Teach us to love others like you love us, and give us the strength and courage to be good even when it is hard or makes us unpopular.

Final song: 'Good Friday' (in *Let God's Children Sing*) or 'I'll sing of a vineyard' (in *Forty Gospel Songs*).

8

A christian passover meal for the family

The central event of the year for a devout Jewish family is the exodus *Hagada, seder* meal or domestic celebration of the passover. It is based upon a tradition going back thousands of years and instructions regarding its celebration are given in Exodus. It is based upon the precept that each Jew in each generation must celebrate the passover as if he personally had escaped from captivity in Egypt and gone out into the desert. It is traditionally an informal occasion: people preparing for a long and arduous journey had no time for unnecessary formality. It is also a joyous occasion—celebrating the freeing of a people from slavery.

By custom, two or more Jewish households combine to share a lamb. Today, a christian family can celebrate a passover with a leg of lamb, inviting another family, relatives, friends and, if possible, some lonely person to join them. We christians are, like the Jews, the children of Abraham and, therefore, we too can celebrate the passover. Our liturgy must express, however, what is new in our own situation. Christ is the new Moses, the fulfilment of the promise, leading the new Israel, God's people, through a new exodus, to the promised land of the kingdom preached in the gospels.

The service that follows is an attempt to achieve such an expression. Just as the Jew in each generation must regard himself as if he, personally, went out from Egypt, so we christians too must relive in each generation the passion of Christ, joining in the second exodus, as if we had died with Christ on the cross and stepped with him out of the tomb. This is one reason why in John's gospel our Lord himself says: 'I am the way, the truth and the life'.

Try to hold the service on Maundy Thursday, or at any other convenient time near to Easter. It is intended primarily for christians without special knowledge of Jewish practice but it will be of special interest to those christians who were brought up in a Jewish home. Such people may like to know that the International Hebrew Christian Alliance (19 Draycott Place, London, SW3) exists and that its activities include the organisation of christian *seders* held at the season of the Jewish passover.

Prepare beforehand the centrepiece of the passover table which is the *seder* dish with its symbolic foods. Buy a traditional *seder* dish at stores selling Jewish religious articles, or use an ordinary meat dish. Decorate it with a metal foil mat, on which the children stick or cut out symbols of the old and new passover, eg a lamb, a pillar of fire, or an empty tomb.

Place on the dish the five traditional foods:

1 A bone of lamb—in memory of the temple sacrifices, reminding us of the lamb of God.
2 A hard-boiled egg—representing the freewill offering made at the temple on each day of the feast. A symbol of birth, it will remind us of the need to be born again in baptism. Eat it at the beginning of the meal before the lamb.
3 Bitter herbs—a piece of horse-radish or *moror* (dried grated horse-radish) standing for the sufferings of the Israelites in Egypt. If desired this can be replaced by horse-radish sauce. It may remind us of the bitter gall given to Christ on the cross.
4 *Charoset* (a paste-like mixture of ground almonds, chopped walnuts, grated apple, a pinch of cinnamon and ginger, the whole moistened with wine). This is thought by some to represent the mortar used by the Israelites in their forced building work in Egypt.
5 Green 'herbs', eg parsley or chicory. These traditionally accompany the paschal lamb and may remind us of the spring and the new life which Christ brings us.
   Provide also:

6 *Matzos* or unleavened bread—now widely available in delicatessens. Place three large pieces on a dish near the leader. The upper and lower pieces are eaten with bitter herbs and *charoset* before the meal. One half of the middle piece (the *afikoman*) is hidden to be looked for by the children and eaten after the meal, while the other is for the eucharist, or to be specially blessed. The hidden *afikoman* may remind us of the hidden action of God's grace.

7 Red wine—four cups are drunk during the service (grape or other fruit juice for the children if desired). Each person has a glass or glasses for the first three but there is a single glass or chalice for the fourth cup, that of Elijah, which is shared.

8 A small bowl of salt water—representing the tears shed in exile, and for us those shed in the garden of Gethsemane.

9 A bowl of water and a towel (for the washing of hands).

10 Children's paintings, collages, mobiles etc, on the exodus theme, which are used to decorate the room.

Allow about ten or fifteen minutes to practise the music (tapes and records can help here). The roast lamb can be cooking slowly in the oven (it will be needed only about thirty minutes after the start of the service). Prepare the rest of the meal in advance, one which does not require attention during the service and which causes the minimum of trouble. This makes it easier to ask the greatest number of people one can fit round the table or several tables put together. Jewish experience suggests that the upper limit should be about twenty-five but for many people twelve or fifteen in all may be a more realistic number. Those who are invited one year should if possible in turn hold their own passover the next year to which they invite people who have not yet taken part.

As it is set out here, the christian passover meal includes a sharing of the eucharist, which is put at a point which is likely to be that at which it was introduced by our Lord himself at the last supper. This has the advantage of showing clearly how the eucharist came into being and how naturally it is related to the passover meal from which it is thought

A CHRISTIAN PASSOVER MEAL FOR THE FAMILY

to be derived. There would seem to be a real advantage to be gained from the occasional celebration of the eucharist in this special setting, thus making a living reality of the continuity of some 4,000 years of Judaeo-christian worship.

If preferred, hold the eucharist separately beforehand, using perhaps the liturgy of Maundy Thursday, or omit it altogether. In either case, leave out the prayers marked * below, and distribute the half of the middle piece of *matzo* without these prayers of consecration. An alternative prayer for the wine is provided in this case. A shortened version of this service is given in our *Liturgy is what we make it* (London, 1967).

1 Preliminaries and the cup of sanctification

With the people seated at table the leader (host or hostess) should remind people that the passover meal is a traditional Jewish celebration with the purpose of recalling and reliving the events of the exodus from Egypt. He should explain that it is celebrated in the home by a family or families because the home, no less than the church (synagogue) can be a sanctuary of God.

Whoever has prepared the *seder* dish now points out the items on it and explains their symbolism. Finally, the leader reminds people that the custom is to drink four cups of wine as a sign of freedom—from bondage for the Jew and from the slavery of sin for the christian. He points out the single shared cup of Elijah, originally an extra one for the unexpected stranger or destitute wanderer, for Elijah was to return, poor and ragged, to herald the coming messiah. This last cup becomes for us, therefore, the cup of the messiah.

All sing: eg 'People of God' (Harvey & Co).
While the hostess lights the candles, all say:
Praise be to you, O God, the source of light.
Leader: Let the light of your presence shine in our homes, sanctify our lives and bring a blessing to all your children. (The leader now asks all the children to stand up.)
All adults: May God bless and guide the children who are with us tonight that they may grow up to be worthy

143

members of the people of God and render devoted service to their fellow men.

Children: Amen.

The first cup of wine is poured out and people hold it in their hands while they say:

Blessed are you, O Lord our God, king of the universe, creator of the fruit of the vine.

Blessed are you, O Lord our God, king of the universe, for you have kept us alive and brought us together again in this season.

The first cup of wine is drunk. The leader washes his hands, dips the 'green herbs' (chicory or parsley) into the salt water and distributes them saying:

Blessed are you, O Lord our God, king of the universe, creator of the fruit of the earth.

He takes the middle *matzo* and divides it into two. The smaller part is replaced between the upper and lower *matzos* and the larger part is hidden by someone as the *afikoman* (for the unexpected stranger). The *seder* dish is raised while he says:

This is the bread of suffering which our fathers ate in the land of Egypt, let all who are hungry come and eat, let all who will come and celebrate the passover. This year we eat it here, but some day we hope to eat it in your kingdom, in the glory of Christ whose power lasts for ever and ever, Amen.

2 The cup of rejoicing and the children's questions.

The second cup of wine is poured out. A child asks the first question:

Why are we gathered here together?

One of his parents or another adult answers it simply, eg:

To eat the passover meal that our fathers ate before they went out from Egypt into the desert.

All: Blessed are you, O Lord our God, king of the universe, creator of the earth on which our food is grown.

Blessed are you, O Lord our God, king of the universe, for you have brought us here again to eat this passover meal of lamb, *matzo* and bitter herbs.

A child asks another traditional question:
Why is this night different from all other nights? Why do
we relax and sing as we eat?
One of his parents or another adult answers it simply, eg:
Because the meal that we eat tonight is the meal that our
fathers ate to celebrate their freedom from slavery and
because we celebrate too the freedom that Christ won for
us on the cross.

Reader: Blessed are you, O Lord our God, king of the
universe who kept your promise to our father
Abraham that his descendants should be as many
as the stars of heaven and his name a blessing
for all peoples.

All: Blessed be he who keeps his promise to his people.

Reader: Our ancestors were exiles in a land not their own.
They were slaves there, oppressed by the Egyptians for four hundred years. But you passed
judgement on their oppressors and set our fathers
free with many possessions.

All: Blessed be he who keeps his promise to his people.

Reader: You led our people for forty years in the wilderness to teach us how to keep the commandments;
you brought us out of Egypt to a rich land of hills
and valleys watered by the rain from heaven,
bringing forth corn, wine and oil with grass for
our cattle, to a land flowing with milk and honey.

All: Blessed be he who keeps his promise to his people.

Reader: You, O Lord our God, spoke to us through your
prophets. You promised to raise a new Moses for
us from among your people to speak your words
and give us your commands. You promised to
send your servant to suffer for us so that our sins
could be forgiven.

All: Blessed be he who keeps his promise to his people.

Reader: You, O Lord our God, when the fullness of time
had come called your people to repent for your
kingdom was at hand.

All: Blessed be he who keeps his promise to his people.

Reader: You, O Lord our God, promise us a new heaven
and a new earth for your word cannot pass away.

145

All: Blessed be he who keeps his promise to his people. The cup of wine is raised.

Leader: It is your promise that has supported our ancestors, as in every generation our enemies rose up against us to destroy us but the holy one, blessed be he, delivered us from their hands. We cried to the Lord, to the God of Abraham, of Isaac and of Jacob, the God of our fathers and he heard us and saw our trouble, our suffering and our oppression. The Lord freed us from slavery as out of Egypt he brought his people. He freed us from sin as out of Egypt he called his son.

All now sing 'My Father was a wandering Aramean' (*Gospel Song Book* p 27, or *Forty Gospel Songs* p 8).

3 The *Dayainu*

The leader recalls one by one the things that God did when he brought Israel out of Egypt. After each phrase the rest reply:

We would have thought it enough.

Leader: If he had freed us from Egypt and not punished our oppressors.

If he had punished our oppressors and not given us their wealth.

If he had given us their wealth and not divided the sea for us.

If he had divided the sea for us and not brought us through it on dry land.

If he had brought us through it on dry land and not drowned our enemies behind us.

If he had drowned our enemies behind us and not led us through the wilderness.

If he had led us through the wilderness and not fed us with manna.

If he had fed us with manna and not given us water from the rock.

If he had given us water from the rock and not brought us to Mount Sinai.

If he had brought us to Mount Sinai and not given us the commandments.

146

If he had given us the commandments and not brought us to the promised land.

If he had brought us to the promised land and it had not been fertile.

If it had been fertile and he had not made us a nation.

If he had made us a nation and not chosen us to be his own people.

If he had chosen us to be his own people and not called us to be a light to all peoples.

If he had called us to be a light to all peoples and not sent his servant to suffer for us.

If his servant had not been the messiah.

If the messiah had not been the son of man.

If the son of man had not been God's own son.

If God's own son had not suffered for us.

If God's own son had suffered and not died for us.

If he had died for us and not spent three days in the tomb.

If he had spent three days in the tomb and not appeared again to his disciples.

If he had appeared again to his disciples and not promised to send the Spirit to us.

If he had promised to send the Spirit to us and not to make all things new.

If he had promised to make all things new and not to come again.

All: We thank you, O Lord, our God, king of the universe, for all the good things that you have done for us, especially for the old passover and the new.

Child (pointing to the lamb bone):

Why do we eat lamb on this night? What does it mean?

His parents or another adult reply:

It is to remind us of the offering that our ancestors made to God on the night that he freed them from slavery, sprinkling the blood on their doorposts so that he should pass over their houses when he punished the Egyptians. It is to remind us that they ate roast lamb that night in haste ready for the journey.

It is to remind us, too, that Jesus Christ offered himself

as the paschal lamb to free us from sin, 'Behold the lamb of God, behold him who takes away the sins of the world.'
Child (pointing to the *matzo*): Why do we eat unleavened bread on this night? What does it mean?
His parents or another adult reply:
To remember that our fathers did not have time to prepare leavened bread before following the call of the Lord and that we ourselves must act like leaven among mankind.
Child (pointing to the horse-radish):
Why do we eat bitter herbs on this night? What does it mean?
His parents or another adult reply:
It is to remind us of the bitterness of the suffering, hard labour and death when our ancestors were slaves in Egypt. It is to remind us too of the bitterness of sin and the sufferings of Christ that brought the human race back to God.

Leader: In every generation, each one of God's people must think of himself as though he personally had just been freed from slavery, for in the bible is written:

> And on that day you will explain to your son, 'This is because of what the Lord did for me when I came out of Egypt.'

And in every generation too each christian must think of himself as though he personally had just died with Christ and risen again with him, for it is written that he said:

> I am the way, the truth and the life. Behold I make all things new. Except a man be born again of water and of the spirit he cannot enter the kingdom of God.

The cup of wine is raised.
Leader: Therefore we offer our thanks, praise, song and adoration, we exalt, bless and glorify him who led us from slavery to freedom, from sorrow to joy, from mourning to rejoicing, from darkness to light, from sin to salvation. And let us sing before him a new song, praising the Lord:

Hallel (Ps 113–118).
All say psalm 113.

The second cup of wine is drunk while all say:
Blessed are you O living God of Israel, your people, creator
of the fruit of the vine.
All say psalm 114 and psalm 115 : 14–18:

4 The bread of life and the bitter herbs
The leader takes the remaining half of the middle *matzo*
from the dish and says:

Leader: Blessed are you Lord God of all creation. Through
your goodness we have this bread, which earth has given
and human hands have made. We offer it to you. It will
become for us the bread of life.

All: Blessed be God for ever.

Leader: We remember that our ancestors ate unleavened bread for seven days each year when the
grain was brought in. They ate only the new
grain without anything old in it to mark the need
for a new beginning. The Christ himself came to
enable us to turn back to you and make a new
start.

All: Help us to make a new beginning.

Leader: We take this bread at the passover so as to remember that when our fathers fled from Egypt
in great haste to start a new life in the promised
land they had no time for the leaven to work.

All: Help us to make a new beginning.

Leader: We remember that when the Christ came he
shared a passover meal with his friends, on the
night before he was betrayed, a meal; just like
we are sharing now.
He took the *matzo,*
just as we are doing now.
Instead of looking back
to the sufferings of the exodus,
he looked forward to death,
a death he freely accepted.

All: Help us to make a new beginning.

Leader: He broke the *matzo*
gave it to his disciples and said:

> Take this all of you and eat it:
> this is my body given up for you.

All: Help us to make a new beginning.

Leader: Lamb of God you take away the sins of the world.

All: Help us to make a new beginning.

> I am not worthy to receive you, but only say the
> word and I shall be healed.

Communion is now given round the table, each person saying to his neighbour: 'The body of Christ.'

(If it is not a eucharist, instead the leader takes the remaining half of the middle *matzo* and distributes it saying:

> Blessed are you, Lord God of all creation, for you bring forth bread from the earth. Blessed are you, Lord God of all creation, for the salvation you have given us.
> Blessed are you for the unleavened bread we eat in remembrance of the freedom you gave our fathers by bringing them out of Egypt.)

After a minute or two of silence the leader takes the upper and lower pieces of *matzo* and distributes them. All eat a piece with a little bitter herbs (horseradish) with *charoset,* saying:

> Blessed are you, O Lord our God, king of the universe, who commanded us to eat bitter herbs to remind us of the need for suffering and service.

5 The meal itself is now eaten, starting with the hardboiled egg.

6 The cup of the promised kingdom

After the meal the children hunt for the *afikomen,* the hidden half of the middle piece of *matzo,* the finder being rewarded. After it is shared out, no more is eaten that day. The third cup of wine is poured out.

All: Blessed are you, O Lord our God, king of the universe, source of all good things. You feed us not only with the fruits of the earth but with spiritual gifts in your loving kindness and mercy.

Supplications

Leader: Remember us before you, as you remember Abraham and our fathers, as you remember the messiah the son of David your servant, as you remember Jerusalem your holy city and as you remember the Spirit that you sent, the source of all kindness and mercy, all peace and life, on this day, the feast of unleavened bread.

> O Lord, our God, remember us
> For the love you bear your people,
> Come to us as a saviour
> Let us share the happiness of your chosen ones
> The joys of your nation
> And take pride in being among your heirs.

(Ps 106 : 4–5)

The leader begins the litany

Leader: The all merciful.

All: May he reign over us for ever and ever.

Leader: The all merciful.

All: May he be praised in heaven and on earth.

Leader: The all merciful.

All: May he be glorified through us for ever and ever, and honoured amongst us to all eternity.

Leader: The all merciful.

All: May he send abundant blessings to this house and upon this table at which we have eaten.

Leader: The all merciful.

All: May he cause us to inherit the day which will be entirely a holy day.

Leader: The all merciful.

All: May he make us worthy of the days of Christ and of the life of the world to come.

Leader: Great salvation he gives to his king and shows steadfast love to his anointed, to David and his descendants for ever. O Lord God, who lived in the city of peace built on the holy mountain, bring peace to all your people.

All: May the Lord give strength to his people and bless us with peace. Blessed are you, O Lord God, king of the universe, creator of the fruit of the vine.

The third cup of wine is drunk.

7 The cup of the anointed one
The leader now pours the fourth cup into the single glass
chalice.
All say psalm 116.
The leader now takes the bowl of water and a towel and
washes the hands of each person in turn saying each time:

Your servant, Lord, your servant am I. In the scroll of the
book it is written of the anointed one that he comes to do
your will.

All answer: If Christ came to serve us, how much more
ought we to serve one another.
All say (or sing) Psalms 117 : 1 to 118 : 4.
All sing (or say) Psalm 136 (Grail psalm card or in *Praise
the Lord*)

Leader: From everlasting to everlasting, you are God. We
have no king but you.

All: God of the first and of the last, God of all creatures, Lord of all generations, you are forever
faithful, you give justice to those denied it, food
to the hungry, and liberty to those in prison. You
restore sight to the blind, make straight the de-
formed, watch over the stranger, and protect the
widow and orphan. You love the virtuous, and
frustrate the wicked, your reign is for ever, and
your throne from age to age.

Reader: Our mouths could be as full of song as the sea,
our tongues shouting with joy like the waves
breaking on the rocks, and our lips as full of
praise as the spaces of the sky. Our eyes could be
shining with light as the sun and the moon, our
hands spread forth like the eagles of heaven, and
our feet as swift as hinds. Even then, we would
not be able to express our thanks to you, O Lord
our God, and God of our fathers. We would
not be able to bless your name for even one
thousandth of one tiny part of the countless good

things that you have done for our fathers and for us.

Reader: From Egypt you redeemed us, O Lord our God, and from the house of bondage you delivered us, during famine you fed us, and with plenty you sustained us; from the sword you delivered us, from pestilence you freed us, and from grievous and abiding diseases you rescued us.

Reader: Do not abandon us, O Lord our God for evermore. Therefore the limbs which you formed in us and the spirit and breath which you breathed into our nostrils and the tongue which you placed in our mouths, they shall give thanks, bless, praise, glorify, exalt, reverence, sanctify and proclaim the sovereignty of your name, O our king.

Reader: For every mouth shall give thanks to you; every tongue shall take an oath unto you; every knee shall bow unto you; and everything upright shall prostrate itself before you, all hearts shall fear you. All our inward parts and organs shall sing of your salvation, according to the word that is written, 'All my bones shall say: 'Lord who is like unto you who delivered the poor from him that is too strong for him, yes, the poor and the needy from him that oppresses him?'' '

Leader: Who is like you, who is equal to you, who can be compared to you the great, the mighty and awe-inspiring God, the most high, possessor of the heaven and the earth? We shall praise you, laud and glorify you, and bless your holy name as it is said of David 'Bless the Lord O my soul; and all that is within me, bless his holy name'.

All: You are God, in your powerful might, great in the glory of your name, mighty for ever and awe-inspiring by your acts, the king who sits upon a a high and lofty throne.

Reader: In the gatherings of countless thousands of your people, of the new Israel, your name will be glorified with joy, O our king, through every generation, for all creatures must give thanks, praise, revere, glorify, honour, exalt and adore you beyond the words of the hymns and psalms of your servant David, son of Jesse.

Praised be your name for ever, O our king. O Lord our God, and God of our fathers, with song and praise, hymn and psalm, strength and sovereignty, victory and power, adoration and glory, blessings and thanksgiving, holiness and majesty from now until all eternity.

All: Holy, holy, holy, . . .

*Leader: Lord, you are holy indeed,
the fountain of all holiness.
Let your Spirit come upon this gift to make it holy
so that it may become for us
the blood of our Lord, Jesus Christ.
He ate a passover with his disciples
like the one that we share tonight
and when supper was ended took the cup.
Again he gave you thanks and praise,
gave the cup to his disciples and said:
Take this, all of you, and drink from it:
this is the cup of my blood,
the blood of the new and everlasting covenant.
It will be shed for you and for all men
so that sins may be forgiven.
Do this in remembrance of me.

Communion is now given round the table, each person saying to his neighbour: 'The blood of Christ.'

(If not a eucharist, the leader instead of saying this prayer takes and blesses the fourth cup before it is passed round: Blessed are you O God of Israel, creator of the fruit of the vine, who gave us new life through your Son.)

Leader: Let us proclaim the mystery of faith.
All: Lord, by your cross and resurrection you have set us free.
You are the saviour of the world.

After a few moments of silence:

All: We have now celebrated the passover according to all its customs and shared together the food and the cup that are your promise of eternal life. May we go on sharing such meals together through the years to come until we see the new Jerusalem, the holy city, coming down out of heaven from God.

All: 'When he comes back' (*Gospel Songbook*), or 'Lord of the Dance'.

9

A eucharist of christian unity

This eucharistic service provides an example of a service that was worked out to meet the particular needs of a specific situation, the merging of a number of denominational renewal groups to form a new body 'ONE for Christian Renewal'. The inaugural conference, held in May 1970 at Swanwick, Derbyshire, was attended by some three hundred people. All the main denominations, including Baptists and Roman catholics, were well represented.

It was the wish of the organisers that the event should find expression in a special act of worship and the service that follows was developed over a period of three months starting from a first rough draft. A succession of inter-denominational groups tried out and improved versions of the service until the final form was reached. Some of the problems encountered are discussed in chapter 6.

The congregation were seated in the chapel in chairs which were arranged in sixteen circles with just under twenty chairs in each and a deacon or deaconess was present in each circle. The circles also formed three groups of five or six each, one in the nave and in each of the side aisles. A table covered with a white cloth stood in the centre of the chapel and some of the deacons brought in and put on it a loaf (cut partly through into sixteen pieces), a jug of wine and sixteen plates and glasses. No one stood at this table. Some of the deacons also acted as readers and coordinators but there was no single 'celebrant'. The reason for this was to avoid the impression being given that the service 'belonged' to any single denomination, the psychologically inevitable result of any single person presiding throughout.

The smooth running of the service was the joint responsibility of the sixteen deacons (of various denominations, clerical and lay, men and women), different people being assigned overall responsibility for coordination at different points (eg how long a silence should last, or when to move on after improvised prayer) and each deacon taking responsibility also for his own circle. It was an occasion of some importance and there was a feeling of *celebration*. The liturgy 'lived' in the full sense of the word. Obviously some adaptations can be made for use in other but similar situations.

1 All say the Declaration of 'ONE for Christian Renewal'.
2 All sing 'As your family Lord' (tune of '*Kumbaya*').
3 Act of penitence
   Scripture reading Mt 5 : 22–26 (Leave your gift at the altar)
   Reader: For our failure to understand and accept our brothers,
   All: Lord have mercy upon us.
   Reader: For lack of faith in your power,
   All: Lord have mercy upon us.
   Reader: For the divided church,
   All: Lord have mercy upon us.
   Reader: For the lack of unity among us.
   All: Lord have mercy upon us.
   Reader: For not doing enough to help the suffering and oppressed,
   All: Lord have mercy upon us.
   Reader: For failing to see you among our fellow men.
   All: Lord have mercy upon us.
Individuals now continue with their own petitions or with periods of silence.
   Reader: Let us now declare together our sorrow.
   All: I confess that I have sinned against you, almighty God,
      and against you, my brothers and sisters,
      in thought, word, deed and omission
      through my own fault.
      We ask your forgiveness in the name of Jesus Christ our Lord.
   Readers: As we forgive the sins of others.
      so in him we have the forgiveness of our own sins.
      Keep us in everlasting life.

4 Scripture readings: Col 1 : 21–28; Mt 10 : 34–39
  Informal discussion of scripture readings with the people
  around.
5 Hymn: 'Holy, holy, holy' (*Ancient and Modern* 160)
6 Thanksgiving

Group 1:   The Lord be with you.

Groups 2, 3: And with you,

Group 1:   Where two or three are gathered together in
             his name,

Groups 2, 3: He is present among them.

Group 1:   Let us lift up our hearts.

Group 2:   Let us raise them up to the Lord.

All: Let us give thanks to God.

Group 1:   It is right
             that we should always
             give thanks to you our God,
             the Lord of history,
             who made us after your own likeness
             and sent your Son
             to free us from the bondage of sin

Groups 1, 2: You have called us out of darkness into light
             to become a chosen race,
             a royal priesthood,
             a holy nation, your own people,
             to make the world anew according to your
              will.

All: And therefore we proclaim your good news
             to the ends of the earth
             and join with all who know your name
             to sing of your glory:
             Holy holy holy. . . .

Group 3:   O Loving Father, you have called us,
             through the baptism we share,
             to accept one another in the name of Christ
             and become your holy people.

Group 2:   Send your Spirit down among us
             gathered here in your name
             that this bread and this wine may become
              for us

               the body and blood of your Son,
               the promise of eternal life.

Group 1:   For he, the night before he suffered,
               took bread and gave you thanks.
               He broke the bread, gave it to his disciples
                  and said:

All: Take this all of you and eat it:
               this is my body which will be given up for
                  you.

Deacons now break bread and take to side tables

Group 1:   When supper was ended, he took the cup.
               Again, he gave you thanks and praise,
               and giving the cup to his disciples said:

All: Take this, all of you, and drink from it:
               this is the cup of my blood,
               the blood of the new and everlasting covenant.
               It will be shed for you and for all men
               so that sins may be forgiven.
               Do this in memory of me.

Deacons now pour wine and take to side tables

Group 2:   Father, we remember that Jesus died for us
                  and rose again,
               to begin a new creation,
               and a church worthy of your name.

Group 3:   May we who share together
               the bread of life and the cup of salvation,
               help to create this true church of Christ,
               new in witness, worship and life.

Reader: May your Spirit guide us in understanding
               what we must do to shape the world
               in the pattern of your love,

Reader: to feed the hungry

Reader: free the oppressed,

Reader: comfort the lonely,

Reader: forgive our enemies,

All: and love our neighbours as ourselves.

Group 1:   May our love for one another.
               and our unity with all men,
               who acknowledge your name,

become for the whole of mankind
a sign of your presence
so that the gospel may be believed
and your glory made known.

All: Through him, with him, in him,
in the unity of the Holy Spirit
all glory and honour is yours,
almighty Father, for ever and ever.
Amen.

7 All sing 'Our Father' (Caribbean version in *Faith, Folk and Clarity* or alternative version in *Prayer, Praise and Protest*)

Reader: Deliver us, O Lord Jesus Christ, from every evil.

Reader: For you said to your apostles
I leave you peace, my peace I give you.

Reader: Look not upon our sins, but on the faith of your church,
and grant us that peace and unity which belong to you,
for the kingdom, the power and the glory are yours,
now and for ever.

All: By our one baptism we are members of the one body.
Then let there be peace among us
so that we may be one also in the Spirit.

All exchange a handshake with their neighbours saying: 'Peace be with you.'

Reader: Let us join in saying:

All: This cup of blessing we bless is a sharing in the blood of Christ and this bread we break is a sharing in the body of Christ. Because we all break and share this one bread, we who are many are one today.

8 Communion

As each person passes communion to his neighbour he or she says in turn: 'The body of Christ' or 'The blood of Christ'.

Silence will then be kept for a while.

Reader: Let us now pray together:
All: Lord, by your cross and resurrection
you have set us free.
We will renew the face of the earth
until you come back in glory.

Deacons now return vessels to centre table

All: The grace of our Lord Jesus Christ and the
love of God
and the fellowship of the Holy Spirit
be with us all now and for evermore.

9 Final song 'Lord of the Dance', Sidney Carter.

10

A eucharist for children

A suitable liturgy of the word should be worked out by the catechist beforehand, preferably with the help of the children. Scripture readings should either be taken from a children's bible or the text rewritten by one of the older children. In the introductory liturgy leading up to the eucharistic prayer good use can be made of singing, mime and visual aids, including children's drawings on the theme chosen for the occasion. This eucharistic prayer is based on one which was worked out by a group of parents and catechists for children of junior school age.

A leader (preferably a priest or catechist who has worked with the children) says:

> God our Father, you are good indeed,
> you give us so many wonderful things.

He then asks the children:

> What has God given us that we like best?
> What shall we thank him for?

If the children fail to respond adequately he says on their behalf:

> You have given us life
> and all that makes life good:
> the people who love us
> and those we love,
> our friends and people who help us.
>
> We thank you Father,
> for the houses we live in

for clothes to keep us warm and dry
for all the new things to discover
for friends to play with
for all the fun we have.

Leader: The best thing of all was
that you sent us your Son Jesus.
He showed us all
how much you love us.
He looked after people
who needed help.
He made sick people well again,
and brought happiness and joy.
He made blind people see again
and fed those who were hungry.
He is here to help us still
and we too can help him
by looking after one another.
We are now going to do what Jesus did
when he ate supper with his friends.
He took bread like this,
broke it and said:
All of you take and eat this
for this is my body given for you.
After supper, he thanked God our Father
and took a cup of wine, saying:
All of you drink of this
for it is the cup of my blood
poured out for you and for everyone
so that your sins are forgiven.
Our Father, we do this
because Jesus told us to
and we remember
that you sent him to us,
to come and live among us on earth,
to die and rise from the dead,
to bring us a new and happy life.
Send us your Holy Spirit
to fill us with your love,
so that we may love others,

as you love us.
Here, Lord, are the bread and wine
that are your body and blood.
Here, Lord, we are,
wanting to help you
by trying to be good
and kind to each other.

All: Together with Jesus and the Holy Spirit
We say to you, Father, how great and holy you are.
Amen.

Leader: As Jesus asked us let us now sing:

All: Our Father (Caribbean version, mimed if possible).

Leader: Our Lord came to bring us peace
Let us all live as friends together.
To show that we are at peace
with one another
Let us shake hands

All shake hands with those next to them.

Communion with a song (eg 'Let us break bread' or 'As your family Lord').

The leader gives a final blessing and then says:

Go in peace to love and serve the living God

All: Thanks be to God.

Final song (one with a good rhythm to which children can clap and dance).

11

Two eucharistic prayers

The need for new eucharistic prayers

The 'eucharistic prayer' is the central prayer often called the 'canon'. The role of new eucharistic prayers is to relate the traditional understanding of the new testament message to the current situation and needs so as to bring the gospel and tradition to life and make them really live for today. New prayers should draw upon both the church's traditional re-sources and good contemporary prayer that has meaning for the twentieth-century christian. How to set about working out contemporary eucharistic prayers is explained in ch 7.

A number of eucharistic prayers were given in previous chapters, and others will be found in *Open Your Hearts* (Oosterhuis). We give two further examples.

Eucharistic prayer of God's love

Leader: We come together in the name of Christ
All: To love and serve God.
Leader: Let us recall that Christ made us God's own people
All: So that we may pledge ourselves to carry out his will.
Leader: Father, we recall that you sent your son
               to bring us into a new relationship of love
               with you and with each other.
               We remember the words of your son
               on the night before he died,
               when he took bread and blessed it:
               and said to his friends:
               'Take and eat this, all of you:
               This is my body, given for you.'
               We remember his words too,
               When he took the cup after supper

gave thanks again and said:
'Take this and drink it all of you:
This is the cup of my blood,
the blood of the new and everlasting covenant
which is to be shed for all men
so that sins may be forgiven.
Do this to remember me.'

All: Therefore, Father, we offer ourselves
through his body and blood
in the name of the risen Christ
and promise again to keep his command
to love you in one another
even as you love us.
Father we know that you love us
because you have given us so much,
because you have given us faith,
because you have given us your Son,
because you have given us his resurrection,
because you have given us life,

If preferred, different people can read different lines of the previous paragraph, and can continue with their own reasons.

Leader: Father we thank you
For Christ who lives among us
through your Spirit
to unite us with one another
so that we will become your people.
May this Spirit of Christ
show us your divine will
and help us to do it.

Reader: Father, we ask that our work here (this evening) may bear fruit.

Here special prayers are offered for those in need of help

All: Therefore, in the peace of Christ,
through him,
with him,
in him,
in the unity of the holy Spirit
giving all glory and honour
to you our Father,

let us show that we are at peace
with one another.

All express their common fellowship by a handshake with
their neighbours, saying 'peace be with you'.

Leader: Knowing your love for us
        We pray (sing):

All: Our Father

Leader: This cup of blessing we bless is a sharing in the
        blood of Christ and this bread we break is a sharing
        in the body of Christ.

All: Because we all break and share this one bread we
        who are many are one body.

Communion is now given

An early christian eucharistic prayer?

John's gospel was one of the latest writings of the new testament, being almost certainly written down only when an
organised church with an established liturgy already existed.
It is at least conceivable that part of the tradition upon which
the gospel writer was able to draw included a eucharistic
prayer and that, in particular, chapter 17 of the gospel may
have been based upon such a prayer. According to J. Marsh
(*The Gospel of St John*, London 1968) the suggestion that
this chapter was composed by some christian prophet as a
eucharistic prayer for use in his church is by no means im-
probable. It is more likely that the prayer was derived from
such a source than from a reconstruction of what people could
remember of the words used by Jesus, or of the substance of
a prayer that he said in the upper room. If so, it would mean
that what the writer of the fourth gospel did was to reset such
a prayer in dramatic form as if spoken by Christ, so as to
provide the seventeenth chapter of the gospel.

What follows is an attempt to reverse what the gospel
writer would have done, and to reconstruct the hypothetical
eucharistic prayer that may have been the source for this
part of the gospel. Probably the best indication of whether
the hypothesis has any basis is whether what follows is effective as a eucharistic prayer.

The usual Pauline consecration prayer has been replaced
by a eucharistic passage from John 6 that is in effect a conse-

cratory prayer. Similarly, a passage from the opening of the same gospel replaces the usual *sanctus* prayer. Unlike most eucharistic prayers, this one does not explicitly contain the theme of thanks. It should be borne in mind, however, that the themes of glory and blessing in Hebrew thought are asking implicitly for the continuance of the blessings of God and are, therefore, an expression of gratitude for them.

Leader: Father, the hour has come:
glorify your Son
so that he may make your glory known
and through the power over mankind
that you have given him
give eternal life to all your people.
And this is eternal life:
that we know you, the only true God,
and Jesus Christ whom you sent.
He glorified you on earth
and finished the work
that you gave him to do.
Now, Father, glorify him
with the glory that he had with you
before the world was made.

All: The Word was made flesh,
he lived among us,
and we saw his glory,
the glory that is his as the only Son of the Father,
full of grace and truth.

Leader: He made your name known
to the men you gave him from the world.
They were yours, you gave them to him
and they kept your word.
Then at last they knew
that everything you gave him was from you;
for he gave them the teaching you gave him,
and they truly accepted that he came from you,
and believed that it was you who sent him.

All: We pray for those who believe:
we pray not for 'the world'
but for those you give to Christ
because they belong to you;
all that he has is yours
and all that you have is his
and in them he is glorified.
Now he is no more in the world
but we are in the world,
and he has gone to you.

Leader: Holy Father, keep those you gave him
true to your name
so that they may be one like you
While he was with them
he kept those you had given him
true to your name.
He watched over them and not one was lost,
except the one who chose to be lost,
and this was to fulfil the scriptures.
Before he went to you,
while still in the world,
he told them these things
to share all his joy with them.
He passed your word on to them
and 'the world' hated them
because they were not of 'the world',
even as he was not of 'the world'.

All: We do not ask you to remove us from the world
but to protect us from the evil one.
We do not belong to 'the world',
any more than he belonged to 'the world'.
Consecrate us in the truth
for your word is truth.
As you sent him into the world,
so he sent us into the world
and for our sake he offered himself,
so that we too might be consecrated in truth.

Leader: For Jesus said:
I tell you most solemnly,

everybody who believes has eternal life.
I am the bread of life.
Your fathers ate the manna in the desert
and they are dead;
but this is the bread that comes down from heaven,
so that a man may eat it and not die.
I am the living bread which has come down from
   heaven.
Anyone who eats this bread will live for ever;
and the bread that I shall give
is my flesh, for the life of the world.
I tell you most solemnly,
if you do not eat the flesh of the Son of Man
and drink his blood,
you will not have life in you.
Anyone who does eat my flesh and drink my blood
has eternal life,
and I shall raise him up on the last day.
For my flesh is real food
and my blood is real drink.
He who eats my flesh and drinks my blood
lives in me
and I live in him.
As I, who am sent by the living Father,
myself draw life from the Father,
so whoever eats me will draw life from me.
This is the bread come down from heaven;
not like the bread our ancestors ate:
they are dead,
but anyone who eats this bread will live for ever.

All: May we all be one, Father,
may we all be one in you,
As you are in Christ and he in you
so that the world may believe that you sent him.
He gave us the glory that you gave him
so that we may be one as you and Christ are one,
with Christ in us and you in Christ,
may we be so completely one
that the world will realise that you sent him

and that he loves them even as you love him.
Father, may we the people of Christ
be with him where he is,
so that we all may see the glory
that you gave him in your love for him
before the beginning of the world.
O, Father, righteous one,
'the world' has not known you
but Christ has known you
and we have known
that you sent Christ.
He made your name known to us.
May we continue to make it known
that your love for him may be in us
and that he himself may be in us.

NB The quote marks round certain occurrences of the word
'world' are an attempt to indicate the deliberate ambiguity
in John's use of it, with both good and bad senses.

Source material

The following list indicates some of the sources of material (mostly moderately priced) that can be used in working out forms of worship, and for further study. Fuller annotated book lists are available from the Family Committee of the Newman Association, 15 Carlisle St, London W1 (*Religious Books for Children, Religious Education in the Home* and *Teenagers and Religion*). The material is available by mail order from Lumen Books Ltd., 21 Chatsworth Gardens, New Malden, Surrey, England.

1 *Song collections*
(* Record available)
*Faith, Folk and Clarity,** *Faith, Folk and Nativity,** *Faith, Folk and Festivity** (ed) Smith. Galliard.
Fine collections of modern and traditional religious folk songs.
*Present Tense** 3 vols. Sydney Carter. Galliard.
The collected songs of an outstanding writer and composer in this field.
Prayer, Praise and Protest (ed) Stephen Church. Mayhew McCrimmon.
The songs of the celebrated Coulsdon folk choir.

2 *Gospel songs*
40 Gospel Songs (ed) Richards. Chapman.
Gospel Song Book (ed) Stewart. Chapman.
Both these books are useful collections.
*Go Tell Everyone** Vanguard.
A selection of songs sung by the Southend folk choir.
Biblical Hymns and Psalms L. Deiss. Chapman.
Grail Gelineau Psalms: 24 Psalms and a Canticle; 36 Psalms and a Canticle.
Some of these are recorded. These settings should be more widely used.

Ten Gospel Songs Richards and Dale. Chapman.
Some of these taken from the *New World* translation of the new
  testament. Estelle White, Harvey & Co, Sacred Heart publica-
  tions. Contains 'The People of God'.

3 *Hymn books*
Sing True (ed) Hodgetts. Religious education press.
A wide variety (with guitar chords).
Songs for the Seventies Galliard (words only and music editions)
  contemporary hymns.
Praise the Lord (ed) Trotman. Chapman.
Ecumenical and mainly traditional.
Sing a New Song Mayhew McCrimmon.
Traditional and modern hymns. A demonstration tape is avail-
  able.

4 *Children*
Let God's Children Sing Sr Oswin. Chapman.
For the 5–9 year olds.
Lord Hear Us Sr Oswin. Chapman.
Primary assembly book.
24 Assemblies for Juniors Bullen. Mayhew McCrimmon.
36 Assemblies for Seniors Cockett. Mayhew McCrimmon.
Worked out by leading catechists, these contain many useful
  ideas.
Children and Confession Heggen. Sheed and Ward.
Contains penitential services for children.
Living in God's Family Wetz/Joyce. Darton Longman and Todd.
An excellent series which includes booklets giving specimen
  services, eg *Confession at Seven and Ten* (no 8) and *Teaching
  the Mass* (no 7)—this gives ten mass themes.

5 *Bibles for children*
Most of the following have simplified text and good illustrations.
A Child's Bible Pan Books. The text is simplified but close to the
  original, and the illustrations are good.
Gospel for Young Christians Winstone. Chapman.
Bible for Children Klink 2 vols. Burke.
Bible Stories for Children Darton Longman and Todd.
This keeps close to the Jerusalem Bible translation.

6 *Services and prayers*
Celebration (3 vols. each covering a season) Galliard.
Ideas for services accompanying *Faith, Folk and Festivity.*
World Alive; News Extra (ed) Banyard. Belton Books.
Anthologies for worship—secular readings with suggested scripture.
Contemporary Prayers for Public Worship; More Contemporary Prayers (ed) Micklem. SCM.
A good selection of prayers.
Worship for Today (ed) Jones. Epworth.
Contains a number of experimental services with comments.
Liturgy is What we Make it O. and I. Pratt. Sheed and Ward.
The present authors' earlier book. Contains a number of services
—agapes, a simple passover meal, celebrations and blessings for
Christmas and Easter etc.
Celebrations H. Haas. Sheed and Ward.
An excellent account of adapting worship to various cultures
and situations.
The Experimental Liturgy Book (ed) R. Hoey sj. Herder (USA).
Gives a number of eucharists and other celebrations.
Open Your Hearts; Prayers, Poems, and Songs Huub Oosterhuis.
Sheed and Ward.
Reflections, celebrations and eucharist prayers by one of Holland's leading poets.
Confession and the Service of Penance Heggen. Sheed and Ward.
Contains several penitential services.
It's me O Lord; The One who Listens; The Shade of his Hand
Hollings and Gullick. Mayhew McCrimmon.
Books of prayers. The first contains informal prayers for all sorts
of situations, the second is an anthology of old and new prayers.
The third is a collection of prayers and reading for times of
sorrow and joy.

7 *The charismatic prayer movement*
Did you Receive the Spirit? S. Tugwell. Darton Longman and
Todd.
An English assessment of pentecostalism etc.
Catholic Pentecostals K. and D. Ranaghan. Deus books (USA).
An account of catholic pentecostalism in the USA by theologically trained leading members who have been in the movement
since its inception.

The Pentecostal Movement in the Catholic Church O'Connor. Ave Maria Press (USA).

A study of the movement from the standpoint of a theologian.

8 *The arts and worship*

(a) *Poetry and prose*

Nothing Fixed or Final Sydney Carter. Belton Books.

Step into Joy Joan Brockelsby. Belton Books.

Two collections of poems of use in liturgy.

Hymn of the Universe Teilhard de Chardin. Fontana.

A eucharist has been based on this.

Faber Book of Religious Verse (ed) Gardner. Faber.

Oxford Book of Christian Verse OUP.

Oxford Book of English Mystical Verse OUP.

Listen to Love (ed) Savory. Chapman.

Anthologies of verse, the last also includes prose.

(b) *Drama and dance*

Leave it to the Spirit J. Killinger. SCM.

An American approach to experimental worship. Chapters on dance, body, time/space, 'metaworship' etc.

Lord of the Dance Bruce and Tooke. Pergamon.

The use of creative dance for the communication of religious ideas.

Jo Jonah; A Man must Suffer and Die Colin Hodgetts. Religious education press.

Contemporary plays, using dance, music, slides etc, on world hunger and on Martin Luther King and racialism.

(Organisations such as Christian Aid have a number of drama-tised scripts available.)

(c) *Architecture and the arts*

Third Millennium Churches P. Smith. Galliard.

An examination of the way new 'church' buildings can serve the needs of the changing christian community, meeting its various social and liturgical needs.

The Secular in the Sacred Brian Frost. Galliard.

A short illustrated account of various developments in the use of church buildings—shared churches, community centres, 'churches without walls' etc.

(The Institute of Religious Art and Architecture, Birmingham University is a good source of information. The SPCK Bookshop, Marylebone Rd, London NW1 has a useful stock of visual aids and records as well as books. Many diocesan catechetical centres have exhibitions of audio-visual aids.)

9 Young people

Tomorrow's People A. Castle. Mayhew McCrimmon.
Practical suggestions for involving young people in the life of the parish, by a priest experienced in this work.

The Pastoral Care of Young People A. Castle. Mayhew McCrimmon.
Useful material on youth masses, vigils, source material etc.

Contemporary Themes in Worship J. Dickson Pope. Galliard.
Such as the elderly, the outsider, the homeless, the use of resources, work.

Tensions 3 vols. Galliard.
Services based on various sources of conflict and tension.

Living—Liturgical Style In *Risk* 5, 1. Youth Dept, World Council of Churches. This gives descriptions of experimental liturgy, including dance, and several scripts of services.

Pray With; Live and Pray Church of England Board of Education.
The former is an anthology of traditional and modern prayer suitable for teenagers, the latter is reflections on life.

Lord make me Truly Human Chapman.
A collection of teenagers' prayers from a Rhodesian racially integrated school.

Citizen Incognito Brian Frost. Sheed and Ward.
Reflections on urban man and his relations to God.

Modern Psalms by Boys. ULP.
See chapter 4.

God is for Real Man; Treat me Cool Man Burke. Fontana
American attempts to make God seem real in the language of the people.

Folk Sound T. Bailey, Galliard.
Today's Sound; Sound for the Seventies Tony Jasper. Galliard.
Approaches to christian education through pop and folk.

10 Modern versions of the bible

New World Testament Alan Dale. OUP.
The Winding Quest Alan Dale. OUP.

Good News for Modern Man Fontana.
The Gospel according to Peanuts Fontana.
The Parables according to Peanuts Fontana.

Of the standard versions the *Jerusalem Bible* and the *Revised Standard Version* are the most useful.

11 *Journals*

Christian Celebration. Quarterly from 10 High St, Gt Wakering, Essex.

An excellent approach to a dynamic liturgy in parish, school and home; articles, reviews and service scripts.

Living Worship. Quarterly bulletin (ed) Michael Lehr and Bernard Braley.

An ecumenical bulletin with articles, service scripts, news of events, reviews. Available from 82 High Street, East Finchley, London N2.

Biblical Index

Index